WRITERS AND THEIR WORK

Isobel Armstrong
General Editor

THREE LYRIC POETS

THREE LYRIC POETS:
Harwood, Torrance, MacSweeney

William Walton Rowe

© Copyright 2009 by William Walton Rowe

First published in 2009 by Northcote House Publishers Ltd, Horndon, Tavistock, Devon, PL19 9NQ, United Kingdom.
Tel: +44 (0) 1822 810066 Fax: +44 (0) 1822 810034.

All rights reserved. No part of this work may be reproduced or stored in an information retrieval system (other than short extracts for the purposes of review) without the express permission of the Publishers given in writing.

British Library Cataloguing-in-Publication Data
A catalogue record for this book is available from the British Library

ISBN 978-0-7463-1111-0 hardcover
ISBN 978-0-7463-1116-5 paperback

Typeset by PDQ Typesetting, Newcastle-under-Lyme
Printed and bound in the United Kingdom

Contents

Acknowledgements	vi
Biographical Outlines	vii
Abbreviations	x
Introduction	1
1 Lee Harwood	11
2 Chris Torrance	49
3 Barry MacSweeney	80
Notes	109
Select Bibliography	117
Index	121

Acknowledgements

For their help and encouragement in the preparation of this book, I would like to thank Lee Harwood, Chris Torrance, Stephen Mooney, Jackie Litherland, Phil Maillard, Terry Kelly, and Isobel Armstrong.

Biographical Outlines

LEE HARWOOD

1939	Born in Leicester. Grew up in Chertsey, Surrey.
1958	Studied English at Queen Mary College, University of London.
1961	Worked as monumental stonemason's mate in Mile End Road. Lived in Brick Lane.
1963	Published *Night Scene*, the first of several magazines, including *Tzarad*, he edited and printed. Visited Tristan Tzara in Paris.
1965	Visited John Ashbery in Paris. *Title Illegible*, his first book, published by Writers Forum (London).
1966	Visited USA, met Frank O'Hara and other poets. *The Man with Blue Eyes* published (New York: Angel Hair Books). Worked at Better Books.
1968	*The White Room* published by Fulcrum Press, London. Moved to Brighton.
1969	*Landscapes* published by Fulcrum.
1970	*The Sinking Colony* published by Fulcrum.
1971–2	Writer in residence at the Aegean School of Fine Arts, Paros, Greece.
1971	Published, with John Ashbery and Tom Raworth, in *Penguin Modern Poets, 19*.
1972	Lived in Boston, USA. Met John Weiners and William Corbett.
1973	Began to work at the Post Office, returned to Brighton.
1975	*H.M.S. Little Fox* (London: Oasis Books).
1977	*Boston-Brighton* (Oasis Books).
1981	*All the Wrong Notes* (Durham: Pig Press).
1983	Lived in Bolinas, California.

1984	Returned to Brighton.
1985	*Monster Masks* (Pig Press).
1988	*Crossing the Frozen River: Selected Poems* published by Paladin.
1998	*Morning Light* published by Slow Dancer Press, London.
2004	*Collected Poems* published by Shearsman Books, Exeter.

CHRIS TORRANCE

1941	Born in Edinburgh, brought up in Surrey.
1957	Worked in solicitors' offices.
1965	Worked as a Council gardener, living in Carshalton.
1968	Living in Bristol. Published *Green Orange Purple Red* (London: Ferry Press).
1969	*Aries Under Saturn and Beyond* published by Ferry Press.
1970	Went to live in the Neath Valley, in mid Wales.
1973	*Acrospirical Meanderings in a Tongue of the Time* published by Iain Sinclair's Albion Village Press.
1975	*The Magic Door*, Book 1, published by Albion Village Press.
1976	Began teaching a creative writing class at the University of Wales.
1977	*Citrinas: The Magic Door*, Book 2, published by Albion Village Press.
1980	*The Diary of Palug's Cat: The Magic Door*, Book 3 (Newcastle: Galloping Dog Press). Cabaret 246 readings started by members of Torrance's creative writing class. Torrance commences ongoing collaboration with musician Chris Vine and the group POETHEAT.
1982	*The Book of Brychan: The Magic Door*, Book 4 (Newcastle: Galloping Dog Press).
1986	*The Slim Book/Wet Pulp: The Magic Door*, Book 5 (Swansea: Stone Lantern Press).
1993	*The Tempers of Hazard,* with Thomas A. Clark and Barry MacSweeney (London: Paladin).
1996	*Southerly Vector/Book of Heat: Further Books of the Magic Door* (Neath: Cwn Nedd Press).
2003	*Wobbly Chair* (Cardiff: Canna Press).

BIOGRAPHICAL OUTLINES

BARRY MACSWEENEY

1948	Born in Newcastle upon Tyne. Left school at 16; joined *Newcastle Evening Chronicle* as a copy boy. Met Basil Bunting, who subbed the paper's financial pages.
1966	Attended journalism course at Harlow Technical College, Essex. Worked on the *Bradford Evening Telegraph* and *Argus*.
1968	*The Boy from the Green Cabaret Tells of His Mother* published by Hutchinson, who proposed him for the Poetry Chair at Oxford.
1969	*The Last Bud* (Newcastle: Blacksuede Boot Press).
1971	Married poet Elaine Randell, worked for the Kentish Times. *Our Mutual Scarlet Boulevard* (London: Fulcrum Press).
1972	*Brother Wolf* (London: Turret Press).
1977	*Black Torch* (London: New London Pride Editions).
1978	*Far Cliff Babylon* (London: Writers Forum). *Odes* (London: Trigram Press).
1980	News editor on the *Evening Dispatch*, Darlington.
1985	Began work as reporter and editor for the *South Shields Gazette*, Newcastle. *Ranter* (Nottingham: Slow Dancer Press).
1993	*The Tempers of Hazard*, with Thomas A. Clark and Chris Torrance (London: Paladin) published and destroyed.
1994	Became partner of poet Jackie Litherland.
1995	*Pearl* (Cambridge: Equipage).
1996	*Zero Hour* published in *Etruscan Reader*, vol. 3 (Buckfastleigh: Etruscan Books).
1997	*The Book of Demons* [with *Pearl*] (Tarset, Northumberland: Bloodaxe Books).
1999	*Postcards from Hitler* (London: Writers Forum).
2000	Died.
2003	*Wolf Tongue: Selected Poems 1965–2000* (Tarset: Bloodaxe Books). *Horses in Boiling Blood: MacSweeney, Apollinaire: A Collaboration, a Celebration* (Cambridge: Equipage).

Abbreviations

WORKS BY LEE HARWOOD

CP   *Collected Poems* (Exeter: Shearsman Books, 2004)

WORKS BY CHRIS TORRANCE

GOPR   *Green, Orange, Purple, Red* (London: Ferry Press, 1968)
ASB   *Aries Under Saturn and Beyond* (London: Ferry Press, 1969)
TH   *The Tempers of Hazard* (London: Paladin, 1993)
MD1   *The Magic Door* (London: Albion Village Press, 1975)
MD2   *Citrinas: The Magic Door*, Book 2 (London: Albion Village Press, 1977)
MD3   *The Diary of Palug's Cat: The Magic Door*, Book 3 (Newcastle: Galloping Dog Press, 1980)
MD4   *The Book of Brychan: The Magic Door*, Book 4 (Newcastle: Galloping Dog Press, 1982)
MD5   *The Slim Book/Wet Pulp: The Magic Door*, Book 5 (Swansea: Stone Lantern Press, 1986)

WORKS BY BARRY MACSWEENEY

WT   *Wolf Tongue* (Newcastle: Bloodaxe, 2003)

Introduction

> The possibilities and excitement of the new rather than the safety of recognition
>
> (Eric Mottram)

For a young poet beginning to write at that time, the 1960s were exciting years to be living. The revolt against social conservatism, in music, clothes, speech, and sex challenged deference to hierarchy and opened up a life of new possibilities. An older generation, brought up in the 1930s, saw the youth as getting out of hand: rock and jazz were held to be sexually permissive. So they were, yet, as Alan Sinfield has said, this left out 'other kinds of excitement'.[1] Poets also were experimenting and a conservative establishment used that word in an attempt to keep control: 'experimental poetry' meant that it was non-legitimate, hole-in-the-corner stuff. Meanwhile some poets quite accurately declared themselves experimental writers: retrieving the meaning of the word to indicate that they were exploring new ways of doing things with language, with unpredictable results.

In the realm of social behaviour, the revolt against conservatism spread to the whole of society and became largely irreversible. The history of attitudes to poetry, however, has been different. A 1950s view of it still prevails today, in public media and institutions in the UK. Or at least this has been the case until very recently: there are signs now that things may be changing. Some mainstream publishers have brought out work by the radical, experimental poets; *Poetry Review*, the journal of the Poetry Society, the most influential national institution for poetry, opened its doors – for a while at least – to non-canonical work; and some English departments, sixth forms and universities, have begun to teach this poetry. But it is still largely unseen and unheard. This is not the place to analyse why this marginalization has been so successful, though the reader will find the elements of an answer in the chapters that follow. The purpose of this book is to present three major poets whose work comes out of the ferment of that period. The aim is to offer openings, ways in, so that a reader, perhaps unfamiliar with that type of poetry, can begin to relate to it and enjoy it, i.e. to find her or his way into it, and go on to further discoveries.

In the first place, the context of this upsurge of new writing, which has been called the British Poetry Revival, needs sketching out. The poet and painter Jeff Nuttall, a key participant in the irruption of new ideas and experiences, wrote one of the best accounts of the various impulses for change, political, cultural, and artistic. His *Bomb Culture* also documents at length the range of artistic actions, from Rimbaud to Dada to Charlie Parker, that challenged the young poet in the 1960s. Dadaism announced the 'principle [...] of the authority of the senses': 'taste, canons of aesthetics, standards of living, philosophical associations, stood in the way of enjoyment, sheer fun'.[2] Nuttall goes on to quote Kurt Schwitters, a German poet who had fled to the UK during the Second World War:

> World needs new tendencies in poeting and
> paintry
> Old stuff is not able to lead further on
> [...]
> You prefer the language, when you understand
> by it things, which everybody knows by
> heart already. We prefer the language,
> which provides you a new feeling for new
> whiskers to come

Inside 'whiskers' can be heard whispers, sounds newly emerging, not heard before, just as the music of Parker, and by extension that of modern jazz, exploded into wild speeds and rhythms and exuberant multiplicity of melody. Lyric poetry did not have to be recognizable in the old terms: self-dramatization in language that set itself up as poetic by holding on to traditional rhythms and socially acceptable voices.

Alongside these artistic inspirations were the cultural attitudes and materials that the disaffiliated members of a postwar generation were adopting as their own and that would become marks of their difference from previous generations. Much of this cultural shift came from postwar American popular culture: comics, country and rock music, films like *Rebel Without a Cause*. Other influences came from Beat bohemianism, including drug experiences that altered perception and time-consciousness. All of these ways of living, briefly indicated, were 'vulgar' from the point of view of the gentry, that remnant of the marriage of the English bourgeois and the landed aristocracy that still marked the summit of social aspiration until the days when Mick Jagger of the Rolling Stones, the 'hard' face of rock in the 1960s, became Sir Mick, and Blairism celebrated the arrival of a new social elite.

The breakthrough into experimental ways of writing, though centred on London, affected young poets throughout the UK. It would have been impossible without the network of small presses and little magazines, which was related to the larger scene of the Underground press, and was facilitated by new, cheap technologies like the Roneo stencil machine which could produce multiple copies of hand- or typewritten text. Bob Cobbing, another key activist of the alternative poetry scene, published a magazine called *And*. In the third issue he wrote:

> The poems and other writings that interest us most are unacceptable to publishers, editors and programme planners. And at least some of the writing in this magazine is utterly unacceptable to almost anybody. That is why we put it in. It seems to us that one of the functions of a magazine that doesn't make a profit is to print stuff which is incomplete, tentative, naïve, idiosyncratic and thoroughly irritating – so long as it has enough life to stand up and answer for itself.[3]

Publications of this type, often on a very small scale, sprang up all over the UK, breaking the stranglehold, i.e. the enforced selectivity operated by commercial publishers who hid their narrow conservatism behind the idea of serving 'public taste', which actually meant *their* taste, formed more often than not by a public school and Oxbridge education. After Margaret Thatcher came to power (1979), the cultural conservatives recouped some of the lost ground.[4] But by then the work was there, some of it among the best modern poetry written in English. The excitement of formal innovation is what distinguishes it from the canonical poets. Unfortunately, most studies of postwar literature, such as Alan Sinfield's, when it comes to poetry, read that period through canonical poets such as Larkin or Hughes. Though it is still hard to get access to the innovative work, current publishing enterprises like Salt Publishing or the Archive of the Now (www.archiveofthenow.com) are helping to make it more widely available.

The three poets presented in this book were members of this parallel tradition, to give it another name. Lee Harwood was born in 1939, Chris Torrance in 1941, and Barry MacSweeney in 1948. Between them there were ties of friendship, shared enthusiasms, common concern with lyrical writing. Lee Harwood, when working at Better Books, would 'put new books by new poets in my pockets', writes Chris Torrance.[5] Barry MacSweeney reviewed Torrance's *Acrospirical Meanderings*, which was dedicated to Lee Harwood, and wrote that for him this book 'makes my real world spiritual, and my spiritual world real'.[6] He and Torrance 'felt close enough to declare ourselves "blood brothers in poetry"'.[7] They were both strongly affected by the music of The Doors and Jim Morrison's lyrics. Harwood and MacSweeney were both excited by French avant-gardist writing. All three found in the intensities of poetic imagination an irreplaceable truth, way outside the repertoire of irony and nostalgia to be found in the establishment poets.

Lee Harwood's pivotal book *All the Wrong Notes* salutes Torrance and MacSweeney, at a time when the sixties are finally ending, as guardians and heroes of the truth of the imagination through the freedom of invention. He denounces what would become the knowledge industry, a phrase that had been used since the early seventies in the USA: 'all the books and maps and knowledge give us too little, leave large blank spaces [...]// [...] Educated Summaries are not worth a spit in hell'.[8] And when, in 'A Poem for Writers', he thinks his way into what it would mean 'To finally pull the plug on the word machine,/ [...] step back into the quiet and darkness', to enter the immediate without unnecessary words, for sheer joy, the name of this is Chris: 'Throw your cap in the air, get on your bike, and pedal off/ down hill – it's a joy with no need of chatter,/ Hello Chris.'[9]

'Contemporary English literature seemed to be very clever, modestly ironic poetry, which was clapped according to how it could manage certain metrical schemes and stanzas and things like that.' That is how Lee Harwood describes the feeling among fellow poets in the early sixties; he adds, 'I think now [1972] that this was a crude view, but at the time that's how it seemed.'[10] The need for a freer, expanded poetic language led young poets to read outside standard conventions: they turned to American poetry (e.g. the Beat generation), French poetry (Rimbaud, Apollinaire, Tzara), and those British poets like Blake, Shelley, Clare, and Chatterton who had been neglected by current fashion. The largest single impact came from American poets, in part because they opened the doors to the others: the poets of the postwar 'Revolution of the Word', centred on New York and San Francisco, had taken up and extended the experiments of the earlier twentieth-century European avant gardists, such as Tzara, Khlebnikov, or Schwitters, as well as rereading English poetry with a new sensibility, as in Allen Ginsberg's visionary reading of Blake which made Blake's words real and immediate. The American poets, such as William Carlos Williams, Allen Ginsberg, Charles Olson, Diane di Prima, among many others, showed that Modernism was not dead. They opened up the language of poetry to a much less restricted range of data and experience than were permitted as the proper subjects for poetry according to British public taste. The British poet Tom Raworth (b. 1939) wrote to the American Ed Dorn in 1961: 'poetry over here is, I think, still a "class" thing [...] There's no flow: no use of natural language. The whole thing is so artificial and contrived [...] Nothing has the power to move.'[11] In particular, he mentions Ginsberg's *Howl* as 'one of the poems that started me off reading more and more of the Americans'. *Howl* included not just what was considered to be unprintable language, but homosexuality, madness, drugs, ecstatic consciousness: the excluded life at the margins of society.

British English was divided, along lines of social class, in ways that American English was not. An essay by the Scottish poet Tom Leonard gives a good idea of what was at stake. Its title, 'The Locust Tree in Flower, and Why It Had Difficulty Flowering in Britain', refers to the American poet William Carlos Williams's 1920s experiments with loosening the connective bonds between words so that the language of poetry could draw more freely on the plasticity of language as actually spoken, instead of being bound by socially correct models. The reason this could not have happened in Britain boils down, says Leonard, to the unchallenged force of class: literature = correct writing = correct speech = education = class/money.[12] To be published in the *Times Literary Supplement*, which belonged to the literary establishment, was not on offer to the poets in question. Poetry was not to move outside the measured tones of educated exchange: the model was Auden, not Basil Bunting.

To use expressions of working-class and impolite speech (like 'fuck'), as later happened with punk rock, was the most obvious stratagem of defiance, yet the bottom line was how to forge a poetic language of the highest energy and aliveness. And this had to be done against the received literary language, i.e. through a critique of it. Raw anger and undisciplined desire were necessary fuel for this critique but had to be part of a larger renewal of poetic forms. Form, in turn, has a political dimension, and includes what is meant by inner self, a key province of the lyric. The received view (still) is that confession constitutes inner truth, hence the continued fashion for the confessional mode in poetry. But the problem is that the statute of confession requires a higher authority whose gaze sees into and authenticates the true self.

Tom Raworth notes the difficulties he had to face once he 'really intended to write the truth': 'it was easy to produce clever little exercises, puns, twistings of words, while it was nearly impossible to capture any emotion or feeling. Then when I started I had all those years of I I I ME ME to wash out. Like the rusty water from the tap at first in a long-empty house.'[13] It was a strong English tradition that lyric poets were supposed to use the first-person pronoun as a mark of sincerity. Fictional characters were allowable in dramatic poetry (e.g. Browning's) but not in lyric unless truth and lies could clearly and properly be distinguished. Lyric poems had to express the experience of an authentic self. Indeed, how far this is still the case the reader can judge by checking the type of poetry published by the *Guardian* and other large-circulation media: the usual formula is an 'I' that remembers. Tom Raworth and Lee Harwood started deploying various and multiple 'Is' that a reader cannot sort into real and unreal. As Barry MacSweeney wrote later, 'What are you doing?/ Telling you lies.'[14] The effect is disconcerting if a reader's idea of truth in literature is someone being true to themself by speaking sincerely, which of course is still the idea of truth promoted in the teaching of poetry at school. Historically, it is a Protestant and bourgeois version of truth, and Dada and Surrealism came as a major release from it. Tristan Tzara, the inventor of Dadaism, was an important catalyst for Lee Harwood. And Surrealism, as a release from the bugbear of truth defined as what you can touch and see – 'facts', as Dickens's Gradgrind insists in *Hard Times* – had similarly been an instrument of release for the Welsh poet Dylan Thomas (1914–53). Thomas's poems locate the fear of intimacy as part of an underlying anxiety about loss and expenditure in sex and death. His early poem 'The Force that Through the Green Fuse Drives the Flower' makes nonsense of the common-sense idea of life as an accumulation of experience. Life in Thomas's poem is sheer exuberant loss. Chris Torrance and Barry MacSweeney similarly abjure any attempt to accumulate time. But the crucial difference is that while time in Thomas is presented through a set of metaphors ('The force that through the green fuse drives the flower/ Drives my green age'), where these metaphors convey but remain themselves outside the flow of time, in the later poets 'force' and hence time is inside words themselves. Metaphor, in Thomas, is still the metaphysical freight of lyric poetry, what distinguishes its language from the everyday. Not so with Harwood, Torrance, and MacSweeney, where poetry is not fenced off from the wild meanders of language as actually lived.

When Harwood explores intimacies of feeling almost too delicate for the voice to sustain, he deploys the hesitancies and gaps of everyday speech, the places where meaning breaks down into the sheer lapse of lived time. MacSweeney contrasts the tenderness of northern speech with the sadistic violence of a certain southern English that knows it has the power to give orders. Torrance's luxuriant language refuses social classification, but by the same token reneges on any preciousness; the sumptuousness does not need to be set apart by posh taste or education – it overflows distinction, and does not equate fineness with refinement. For all three, the work of imagination is distributed through the language, though unevenly, according to its use by different social classes: it is not a question of adopting, modishly, the speech of one particular group, in order to write either 'intellectual' or 'street-wise' poetry.

But who authorizes the poet? What gives him legitimacy if it is not to be the use of specialized and usually high-sounding language that traditionally is associated with the lyric? As with other poets of the British Poetry Revival, the three presented in this book do not look to traditional poetic language to consecrate themselves as poets. For them, to become a poet is, on the contrary, an act of self-creation that does not need the authorization of those who consider themselves the owners of tradition. Rather than being an easy way out, this meant confronting the obscure and intricate taboos and inertias that get in the way of writing: the poet's inner struggles with the elusive figures that block, deceive, but also release – figures that possess but cannot be possessed, whose ancient name was Muses and more modern one Imagination. The American poet Robert Duncan's poem 'Often I am Permitted to Return to a Meadow', published in 1960, offers a scenario that dramatizes that situation:

> as if it were a scene made-up by the mind,
> that is not mine, but is a made place,
>
> that is mine, it is so near to the heart,
> an eternal pasture folded in all thought
> so that there is a hall therein
>
> that is a made place, created by light
> wherefrom the shadows that are forms fall.
>
> Wherefrom fall all architectures I am
> I say are likenesses of the First Beloved
> whose flowers are flames lit to the Lady.[15]

This, of course, is not permission as in lifystyle, accent, 'slapping a back or two' in the literary world, or writing in the expected style. Poetry gives itself permission, through discovering the necessary forms of imagination and affect, fictive but true. Duncan takes imagination to be an inward yet at the same time outward figure, created yet also received by the writer. As well as being its own architecture, in other words self-creating, it is shaped by an archetypal figure (the 'Lady'). This combination of a source of truth, place of deepest feeling, and a mythic *anima* figure, constitutes a more traditional Romantic position than one can find in the three poets under discussion. In their work these elements take a more dispersed and problematic form. Instead of seeking the sources of inner feeling, their poems open language to forces that come from outside: sometimes dark, uncreating forces. At the extreme, as in some of MacSweeney's poems, or in *Lud Heat*, by Iain Sinclair – a poet (though now better known as a novelist) who has published Torrance and written on MacSweeney – the traditional movement of the lyric poem, radiating outwards from a light-source, is reversed. The lyric scene is invaded by damage, historical and psychic. The poem spits in the eye of the reader.

Behind the idea of the lyric as authentic self-expression lies a narrow reading of English poetry. If we go back, historically, to Elizabethan poetry, the lyric could be densely social and political in its language, just as MacSweeney's is. The word lyric refers among other things to song: a condensation of language to the point where it begins to sing, where tone, expression of emotion, becomes music. The meaning, in other words, is inseparable from the play of sound. The poem thus occurs between speech and music, open to the power of both. The highest embodiment of music in contemporary British poetry had been the work of Basil Bunting, who defined poetry as 'lines of sound drawn in the air'. Bunting included a Scarlatti sonata in his reading of his long poem *Briggflatts*, as an intricate counterpoint to the verbal music. The music the three poets of this book engage with is that of the later twentieth century. With MacSweeney's *Odes*, the highly condensed phrases may be compared with Jim Morrison's lyrics for The Doors. In Torrance's poems, the slow saturated notes combined with spare phrasing and tight swerves recall the music of the jazz pianist Thelonius Monk, especially in solo mode.[16] The breaks and silences of Lee Harwood's language follow the modern jazz principle, initiated by Charlie Parker, of creating montage rather than continuous melody.

All three poets take us close up against the real: to quote Paul Evans, fellow poet and close friend of Lee Harwood, 'an exchange' takes place because the writer does not 'draw or tear a hole in the world', i.e. does not use language which cuts up, orders, and labels conveniently.[17] There is in all of them – though not all the time – an interchange with the world which is as unselective as can be achieved. Their aesthetic orientation is similar to the adoption of open systems by visual artists in the late 1960s and early 1970s: the work of art as an open system, in constant and varied interchange with what is outside itself, i.e. the gallery, the public, the city, recalling Shelley's 'unremitting interchange' with the universe as condition of the poet.[18] In these poets, the result is a poetry which breaks up the recognizable, i.e. socially synthesized world, and opens itself to what emerges outside or in the interstices, i.e. to desire and to the cosmos. This is like what happens in Blake's ironical picture of Newton gazing fixedly at the geometrical tidyness of his compasses while matter seethes in unruly fashion underneath and behind him. Instead of a world made of quantities that can be shifted about at will as money can, a language which breaks down the very categories which permit consumer society to dominate and, having pulverized appearance, lets it surge up again transformed.[19] Instead of the lyric as an expression of yearning that can be accommodated to the status quo so that reader and writer can go on living as before, poetry which spits in the eye or pulls out the rug. The way it is done may require MacSweeney's anger, courage, and innocence, but equally may follow Harwood's standing in softness and doubts, or Torrance's humour and his sharp but unfocused eye.

1

Lee Harwood: Embracing Uncertainty

> The effort is to find the sounds, the words and the syntax which will allow the poem to be heard – above all that the words shall not be too heavy, too pretentious: that there shall be an area of silence; there the poem lives if it lives.
>
> (George Oppen)

Lee Harwood was born in Leicester in 1939. After studying English at Queen Mary College, University of London, he did a variety of jobs, including working as a stonemason's apprentice, and at Better Books in Charing Cross Road, an alternative bookshop run by Bob Cobbing. In the 1960s he started up a poetry magazine: 'there *were* no magazines then', he comments, 'I started doing magazines in 1963, the reasons being: [...] the magazines that existed were so conservative that one wouldn't even bother to send stuff, as you knew it wouldn't get you anywhere. Suddenly a little bulb lit in your head and you said "Gosh, I can do it myself!"'[1] In the sixties, he writes in an autobiographical note, 'In Britain, with the giant antibomb marches organised by the Campaign for Nuclear Disarmament, the eruption of "pop music" and "youth culture", as it's now known, all seemed possible. The barriers, the class system, the narrow introversion in the arts – all seemed to be collapsing.'[2] Among the writers who had strongly affected him were Ezra Pound, Tristan Tzara, Jorge Luis Borges, John Ashbery, André Gide, William Carlos Williams, and Frank O'Hara. What particularly interested him in these writers became a characteristic of his own work: the 'ability to show coexisting worlds, or rather, coexisting realities'.[3]

His early poems revel in the 'made-up' quality of any speaking 'I' and of any scene described. Moreover, they give no reliable 'here' and 'now' from which we can measure the distance to a 'there' and a 'then'. The result is an intermittent uncertainty about where we are; the present seems permeated by other persons or places. And yet the poems make deeply intimate statements and are concerned with how to speak the truth. 'As your eyes are blue ...', first published in 1966, is made up of simple phrases:

> As your eyes are blue
> you move me – and the thought of you –
> I imitate you.
> and cities apart. yet a roof grey with slates
> or lead. the difference is little
> and even you could say as much

(CP 28)

Yet some time during the reading of the second line, the first word, 'as', starts to produce an uncertainty: does 'as' mean because, or is it establishing a similarity, between the way 'your eyes are blue' and the way 'you move me', in my thoughts? Thoughts which amount perhaps to becoming the other by imitating them, the lover. This uncertainty about just where the speaker is placing himself, just how close to the lover, is accompanied by a doubt about how much 'difference' there is between the scene that each one inhabits, in separate cities. In this and other poems the uncertainties can also manifest themselves as gaps, where a sentence does not finish, or a typographical space is left in the middle of a line, as in 'Linen':

> touching you   like the
> and soft as
> like the scent of flowers and
> like an approaching festival

(CP 144)

It is a method of incompletion, which makes the working assumption that sharp, 'realistic' focus may not be the most accurate approach, and says to a reader how do *you* imagine that ... ? Uncertainty, instead of being a problem to be resolved in order to survive – think of doing an IQ test or describing yourself in a job interview – becomes an entry, a way of starting to enter the poem's field. What he writes about the poetry of John Ashbery reveals his own sense of the how the poem composes a world: 'half-finished thoughts and sentences which, as he says, is "the way we communicate [...] the way experience and knowledge come to me, and I think to everybody"'.[4]

Softness is a recurrent mood in this early poetry, inviting a reader to enter a relationship with the poem such that the usual routines of self-possession are suspended. The poem 'White' begins: 'It all began so softly and white was the/ colour that showed the most dominance' (CP 83). The whiteness gives the quality of a surface, and the softness one's relationship with it: a contact that brings the sense of seeing into the realm of touch, and which extends to the world outside the poem. This is rather like leaving the cinema after a good film, and finding the streets outside changed, as if the film were still running. The poems share with film the fact of making a visual world available to touch, the haptic or touch-oriented character of film being the mode of its kinetic effect upon the body. Everything in the poem becomes available to this sense of touch and movement, of the body responding to surfaces and spaces.

The first section of 'White' continues:

> It all began so softly and white was the
> colour that showed the most dominance
> In fact – it was a glorious white
> This meant that the toy soldiers had to all be rearranged;
> confusion on all levels and 'no one was really prepared'
> My arms were no longer tired – the rest had been good

'Softly' invites a suspension of boundaries. Less important than who the subject is – which is left vague – is the uncertainty of any boundary between self and other, or at least the fact that no such boundary is given to the senses. Instead of ordering space according to the perspective of an observer in a fixed position, the last three lines offer a non-organized and non-centred space. That feeling is enhanced by the childhood atmosphere of the scenario: the malleability and unfocusedness of the child. At the ordinary level of adult perception, it is not clear what relationship there might be between 'my arms were no longer tired' and 'the toy soldiers' and the 'confusion'; the statements do not add up to an organized scene: especially, there is no image of the body and no definite location of it. Yet the perceptions and sensations are perfectly vivid; indefinacy at one level does not prevent high definition at another.

After the initial mention of the colour white, the poem has moved into narrative. How does the use of narrative relate to surface? Consider the way the second section begins:

> It was a happy occasion
> but you were so surprised to see the same flags still hanging
> limply from the long balcony of the state apartments

A previous time is mentioned ('the *same* flags *still* hanging'), and the 'you' gives the experience a subject. The address to a 'you', even though not a clearly defined person, brings the poem's action into a present, a present shared with someone else, even if the other addressed might in some way be the speaker themself.

A few lines further on, the poem returns to the theme of colour and surface; the white is now white paint: 'The paintings would have to be winter landscapes/ and this means lots of white paint'. 'Paintings' defines a space, consisting in 'winter landscapes', and this localizes the colour white. The mention of 'paintings' also delineates a space by implying a frame or frames; a space that is both seen and made, both a scene and the making of a scene (with paint). The line that follows brings an unexpected change of level: 'I've bought it for you already. he said "look in that cupboard"'. The time frame has shifted, from the indefinite past contemplation of the paintings to an immediate and punctual present. The unconventional punctuation[5] enhances the interplay of time and framing. The full stop after 'already' has an ambiguous status: does it indicate a break in sequence, making 'he said' a shift to another frame, which gets filled with the quoted statement 'look in that cupboard'? Or, given that the full stop is not followed by a capital letter, its authority thus weakened, does not 'he said' also tend to frame the previous 'I've bought it for you already'? In that case, there would be no difference of status between the two utterances, and yet, surely, a difference is indicated by the way the second one is framed by speech marks, a device which gives it a greater degree of directness and thus presence? Two surfaces have been presented to us, which are the same and yet not the same – like adding white to an already white canvas. The softness is therefore to do with the way that varying degrees of definition or sharpness exist at the same time or in the same space. It is the simultaneous definacy and indefinacy, focus and non-focus, that gives the poetry 'a pearly, soft-focus quality,' in John Ashbery's apt phrase in his foreword to *Crossing the Frozen River*.[6]

Instead of using simple location, in one time and one place, Harwood's poems shift without warning between different times and places. In any one poem there can be a variety of different frames. Framing implies degrees of connection with what is outside the frame, 'offscreen' in film language. In narrative this effect is usually called implication, and Harwood's writing, especially in the earlier poems, often draws attention to it, as with the beginning of a poem called 'The Paint Box':

> What did you do? We all know how tired
> you were, but you did, didn't you?
> I mean the formula can be turned most ways
> and it's only a matter then of local colour
> to give *that* touch of distinction.
>
> (*CP* 98)

The *what* the other did, the content of the action, is not stated, and attention shifts towards the action as such. That change of framing continues in the third line, with the talk of a 'formula': attention has drifted from the content of stories and scenes to the act of making them distinct – through use of 'local colour'. This is, literally, a question of painting; and the mention of 'canvas' and 'tubes' draws reading into the time frame of the making of the painting:

> The surface then appeared different –
> but under the paint?
> Canvas was universal – everywhere.
> The tubes of paint were so fat
> and funny, as they didn't matter so much.

What was under the paint is a characteristically Harwood question: in other words, what was/is behind the scene, outside it? The answer given is slightly mysterious: how could canvas be 'everywhere'? How could it have no boundary? And certainly there's no resolving the question by resorting to abstract ideas – the 'tubes of paint' are too physical for that and, indeed, they bespeak an implied question: what produces the scene physically, what action and what material?

Yet 'The Paint Box' keeps, for the time being, to the past as its tense:

> It was 'the rose mist floating down
> on the white mountain crags'
> that was in everyone's mind.
> The poem was printed out like a neat label
> and stuck below the picture.

A rather conventional poem 'was' printed underneath a picture – a more or less kitsch scenario – well, OK ... We've been here before, haven't we? a reader may think: 'Yes! And it's now one more poem' – framed and neutralized. Yet the ending of 'The Paint Box', having offered the complacency of easy recognition, pulls the rug from under it, by asking just what the 'here' of 'been here before' is, just what makes that the case:

> That's funny, isn't it? or maybe
> it's not so funny, but scary instead.
> I mean the whole routine of bare
> canvas and the paints all squeezed out
> on the palette and then it's just for someone
> to step out and say 'GO' in a loud voice.
> And the day goes by in slapping noises
> as more and more paint is used up.

Reading has by this action ceased to be reading *about* a given theme or object; 'about' implies the ability to encompass something, but the 'slapping noises' as paint goes on do not represent anything, they are whatever has to happen before there is a scene or objects. The noises are moreover not represented time but real time; the canvas has no boundary, there is no frame to hold on to. Fiction and the real have become indistinguishable, as have the making of the poem and the reading of it. Of course, as a reader one will tend to step back, and make of the poem read a finished piece of knowledge, a recognition. The poem 'The Other Tiger', by Borges, one of Harwood's favourite authors, has the real tiger in the jungle always eluding the tiger in the poem, because as soon as the tiger is inside the poem it becomes a fiction and by the same token ceases to be the tiger of flesh and blood. Harwood's poem is like an inside-out version of Borges's: it keeps taking us back to a point where real time invades the time of reading, whereas in Borges's, reading repeatedly annuls real time.

If there is a point at which the 'slapping noises' of paint become the real itself, this poem shares with 'White' that strange switching of levels: from the frame that is necessary for a graspable theme to exist, to what has to be in place for that frame itself – or any frame at all – to exist. And this 'what has to be in place' cannot be fully known or encompassed – unless one happens to be a Platonist and believes in the existence of ideal, unalterable, and eternal Forms which precede human perception and indeed make it possible.

Harwood's approach shares with Modernist painting a need to experiment with the effects of framing and surface as such. Kazimir Malevich's Suprematist painting of 1918, *White on White*, consists of a smaller white square within a larger one. The fact that the smaller square is not aligned with the first one but is slightly tilted, and that it has a slightly different shade, makes a viewer aware of movement and of different degrees of saturation. Those concerns continue in the work of Abstract Expressionist painters such as Mark Rothko (e.g. *Ochre and Red, on Red*, 1954), Barnet Newman, and Ad Reinhardt (e.g. *Red Painting*, 1952), where there can be a radical uncertainty as to whether one is seeing two shades on top of each other or a single more saturated one (more saturated than a previous or remembered red, which brings time into the painting). With his large canvases, Newman wanted viewers to stand sufficiently close for them to feel they were inside the painting. These moments when painting and background become the same may be compared with Harwood's creation of radical uncertainty about the borders of the poem. Why did he need this?

The question can be generalized to what is necessary for there to be a poem at all. In the poem 'Landscapes', the act of reading becomes involved in the composition of a landscape: land features (ridges, valley, dark pine forest, etc.) are given that, by virtue of thematic coherence and visual consistency, make up an image, which is also a picture, through the fact that a space is filled and by the same token framed. The poem then goes on to tell of a memory of a picture in the National Gallery, Constable's *Weymouth*, and then to a narrative ('the horsemen are riding through the forest' (*CP* 103)). Various space frames and time frames are brought into play, and reading probes their differences. Yet the way memory works in the poem is surprising. The difference between then and now, which memory usually plays upon, gets eroded: 'my memory of this small part of the/ National Gallery surprises even me,/ & maybe only I know how inevitable it all is'. Why 'inevitable'? Subsequently the narrative of the horsemen goes through a switch of levels: 'Somehow the action has at last gone beyond/ the painting and this is for real.' When this happens the act of reading is not able to assign a definite boundary between the painting and the real. However necessary such a boundary may be for a reader's philosophy, it is here not available: this for Harwood makes the territory of poetry. There follows a strange moment of passivity, strange in the light of Harwood's clear concern that a reader should be 'an active co-producer' of his poems:[7]

> But there can be no self-flattery on this account
> – it has all been decided for us.
> The illusions of freedom are at last
> shown to be so obviously ridiculous that
> most people cry at this point.

Why, or how, is there no freedom? Surely awareness of space and time frames would allow us to move inside and outside the scene at will?

It might be argued that Harwood is pointing up a limit to a reader's freedom: your freedom vis-à-vis the work of art is not unlimited, you cannot do anything you like with it. But the way the poem continues suggests that that is not the point at issue: we are given a sequence of short pieces of narrative where a speaker and an other, addressed in an intimate tone, finding themselves 'outside' the painting, are involved in a parting: 'What is left is a canvas & paints/ and a little time for distraction before the event./ It is not so much a justification – but saying/ "Goodbye" now appears irrelevant.' The sense of there being 'little left to say', which at first seemed to derive from the painting ('it has all been decided for us'), now arises from an event in life itself, a parting between lovers. An actual embodied reader, as opposed to an abstract and ideal individual, cannot move inside and out of the boundaries of this painting or this poem simply 'at will', since the boundaries become coextensive with those of living: it depends on what you are doing, and doing can have no complete boundary. Harwood is interested in the poems that a person is inside of in living, and not the restricted definition of Poetry: instead of poetry which marks off its terrain with easily recognized signs of literariness, such as metaphors, regular metre, and rhyme, a poem whose boundaries elude clear demarcation. The relation between poetry and the actual then becomes open, but also necessary, because the poem partakes of the same process by which any scene might come about.

But there is more. A passage inside quotation marks, which answers the statement 'there is little left to say', follows:

> 'I did care, & the love I claimed
> was & still is the miracle that continues
> to astonish me. I love you.
> It is only that death has forced
> me into obeying its commands.
> I am powerless and in its power.'

The meanings of 'inevitable', 'it has all been decided for us', and 'illusions of freedom' now resonate with death – with a condition that has no outside and, by the same token, is not an event in life.[8] Here there seems to be a kind of answer to the question what is outside the poem or what precedes it and makes it possible. A condition in which there is little or nothing to say *about* an event *inside* the poem now begins to mirror and echo a condition which governs the poem itself, this particular poem that is becoming one through the actual reading of it. Reading thus generates the question: what is that outside which drives the poem and gives the shape of its necessity? A landscape, a painting, a narrative of horsemen, and a parting of lovers produce a sense of the inevitable as that which one is inside of: not fatalism but the discovery of limits.

If Harwood uses spatial frames to distinguish outside and inside, distance and closeness, and time frames to separate abstraction from immediacy, represented time from real time, there is also, as we have seen, a way in which his poems dissolve the frames. This may be 'scary', and death may be the final content of that fear, but the dissolving can also generate pleasure and happiness. This is the case with 'The Final Painting', where the word 'final' gathers together both sets of feelings. It tells of the past movement of a white cloud over the land yet 'the cloud in the blue continues to move – nothing is limited by the canvas or frame – ', and this is linked with a pleasurable emergence into open space:

> The white cloud passes a shadow across
> the landscape and so there is a passing greyness
> The grey and the white both envelop
> the watcher until he too is drawn into the picture
> It is all a journey from a room through a door
> down stairs and out into the street
>
> (CP 107)

The ending of the poem has the painting dissolving into its surrounds: 'The whole painting quietly dissolved itself/ into its surrounding clouds'. The word 'quietly' enhances the inherent joy. If, say, the word were *slowly* dissolved', then attention would be drawn into an appreciation of time lapse; a reader would imagine herself to be standing outside the dissolving. 'Quietly' does something else, it brings into the field of attention a dissolving into quietness, and at the same time dissolves attention itself into that silence, which is visual substance.

If one stands back to consider the poem's various depictions of how its own surfaces come about, one could say it begins with a sense of an expanding frame ('nothing is limited by the canvas or frame'), then shifts to 'the watcher [...] drawn into the picture', and that its next move is to picture a group of 'watchers' inside the frame ('people in overcoats on a hillside/ and the line of clouds above them'). Then, there is the idea of a limit to the act of saying: 'It is beyond spoken words what they are/ silently mouthing to the sky.' Yet 'There was no mystery in this – only the firm/ outline of people in overcoats on a hillside.' 'Mystery' is not allowed to label the picture, to offer a stance that would reduce its clear outlines – to a romantic vagueness, for example. To imagine, instead, seeing the picture from inside it would render all boundaries uncertain, and take reading towards a condition where there is only one surface, albeit discontinuous. Reading, as an act of the imagination, would become one with the surrounding world, everything potentially would enter it. That everything might enter in this way, makes the poem open to the incalculable: 'mysterious' is perhaps not such a bad word to describe this sort of effect.

Or you could say: there is no palpable boundary to imagination, only its surfaces are palpable. To say that is a proposition. As the early Wittgenstein wrote, 'Propositions can represent the whole of reality, but they cannot represent what they must have in common with reality in order to be able to represent it [...] What *can* be shown, *cannot* be said.'[9] The condition of saying things *about* a poem has to share the same condition as the poem – otherwise what one says will be about something other than the poem. There is an outside to what can be said about the poem, and it is *that* outside that the poem addresses. Whatever is proposed about a poem does not encompass it. 'The Final Painting' shows how just as every inside produces an outside, every outside becomes an inside of something else – that is, until the final boundary, or 'the final painting', is reached and there emerges a single, strange surface that breaks away from a world composed of boundaried subjects and objects.

The way Harwood's poems sound upon the ear is a vital part of their effect upon a reader. Like Torrance and MacSweeney, he uses open form; instead of following a regular metrical pattern, such as the iambic pentameter, with its ten syllables and five beats per line, open form means finding the shape and rhythm appropriate to the subject matter. Ezra Pound and other Modernist poets made this their principle in the early twentieth century, though the usual term 'free verse' is not a good description of it, since freedom from regular patterns, including rhyme, was simply a precondition for the demanding task of creating precise patterns of sound appropriate to the materials in hand. Ezra Pound's maxim, 'compose in the sequence of the musical phrase, not in sequence of a metronome',[10] offers a good summary of Modernist practice; it makes the phrase into the basic unit of composition, rather than the 'foot' (the iambic foot, di-dum, consists of an unstressed syllable followed by a stressed one) or the line, e.g. of eight or ten syllables. The implication of following the shape of 'the musical phrase' is that each phrase has its own music – its own pattern of sound and its own duration. This approach to composition had by the 1950s been abandoned by the mainstream of English poetry, particularly by the influential group of poets known as the Movement, of whom Philip Larkin is the best known and Andrew Motion, the current poet laureate, a follower. This has had the long-term result of producing an anti-Modernist expectation of poetry in the minds of the vast majority of people who still read poetry after leaving school. The usual assumption is that Modernism is dead: poetry needs to be less difficult and more 'popular'.

Behind the work of Lee Harwood is the revolution in American poetry from the mid 1950s to the early sixties: the revival of Modernist ways of writing, especially among those known as the New York School of poets, which includes John Ashbery and Frank O'Hara. Robert Creeley's maxim, 'that form is never more than an *extension* of content',[11] serves as a fair summary of the new wave of experimentation. It took Pound's 'compose by the musical phrase' further by opening up writing to all types of patterning, e.g. to rhythms of film or jazz. In Harwood's own reading of the early poems, on *Landscapes*, the Stream Records LP issued in 1969, he tends to pause as much in the middle of phrases as at the end of them. The listener picks up a pattern of intonation that is not based primarily on the phrase but on something else. Let us consider some examples from 'The House'. The pauses range from the almost imperceptible (a slight catching of the breath, a minimal silence) to an unmistakable halt which interrupts both the flow of sound and the sense of the phrases. The extract that follows, which comprises the first ten lines of 'The House', is printed conventionally in the book, with the left margin justified and with consistent single spacing between the lines. I have marked the lesser pauses in Harwood's reading with a single vertical line, and the more substantial halts with two such lines.[12] Clearly, a notation which captured all the subtleties of the reading would, as with a score for musical performance, need to use several types of mark.

> The rain over the hills || – the shades of blue and grey
> in the clouds | on the horizon || with evening coming –
> The house || is on the outskirts of the town; ||
> and the view is something | unknown in the capital ||
> and these colours in the clouds || are meaningless there. ||
> It is | different – a horizon which is formed by |

> a line of | green hills and a solitary | tower. ||
> It's all like | the early landscape in the city gallery. ||
> And this question of | painting and vision |
> and which seems the more real | is fascinating –
>
> <div align="right">(<i>CP</i> 101)</div>

The longer breaks, which I have called 'halts', tend to occur at the place where phrases end; they are sometimes marked by punctuation and quite frequently coincide with the end of the typographical lines. In other words, these longer breaks are placed where there are completions of meaning. The procedure is conventional, and makes the grouping of words coincide with the rhythmic shape (the only exception is the break after 'The house' in the third line); the meaning feels transparent because grammar, sense, and rhythm tend to line up with each other. The shorter pauses, however, work differently. They tend to break the phrases, cutting across the conventional patterning, with unexpected intervals. Take lines 6 to 8: the natural phrases 'It is different', 'a line of green hills', 'a solitary tower', and 'It's all like the early landscape' are all cut by short pauses in the middle, which seem like intervals in the stream of meaning. They suspend the sense of the phrases and each time there's a small shift of tone and feeling. These brief pauses are not like the hesitations of someone searching for a word. In their effect they resemble the way in which one can hear several voices in these poems. Had they been indicated typographically, say as follows,

> It is ... different – a horizon which is formed by
> a line of ... green hills and a solitary ... tower.
> It's all like ... the early landscape in the city gallery

it is likely that someone listening to the recording with the text in front of them would take the dots as gestures of someone wanting to convey uncertainty. This would take away the effect of slight strangeness. It should also perhaps be added that, as already suggested, the short pauses are not uniform in length; some of them are almost imperceptible and therefore signalling them with three dots would be over-emphatic.

The breaking of phrases has a bearing on the relation between rhythm and meaning. If prosody predicts that certain rhythmic figures will repeat, its result is a horizon of expectation: a reader is waiting for the completion of a recurrent pattern. If one listens out for what is the most familiar pattern in English poetry, the eight-syllable four-beat marching rhythm of the ballad, something that can be heard not only in most poetry offered in public, but also in a large number of pop lyrics, there the completion of a line coincides with the completion of a phrase. However, Harwood's brief pauses, as Phil Maillard suggests, make 'a kind of shared drama with the reader, where there is an implied effort needed to "make it" from one phrase to the next, and a prosodic relief when the pause is successfully negotiated'.[13]

The brief pauses cause words to group together according to slight changes of intonation, and these have an intimate relation with the breath. In fact they produce intimacy; through the perturbation or turbulence they cause by getting in the way of clear meaning, they convey intimacy in the sense of the closeness of the body of another. Yet his is not the expression of a known and recognized other as in the idea of confession, when someone 'bares their soul'. What is expressed is not even a voice as such, since those small variations of tone are what a voice is put together from, they are what allows us to receive a particular range of intonation as the characteristic expression of a person. In other words, they are the raw material from which a personal voice is made, and they engender a sort of floating intimacy. It is not a question of making the private public, but of opening up what makes up the private self in the first place. Like his dissolving of visual frames, Harwood's use of tonal variation causes conventional boundaries to become porous. Intimacy drifts across the limits of the private individual, and this in turn cuts across the ordinary rhetoric of speaking where speaking is taken to be the expression of an individual. The speakers in the poems cannot easily be fitted into a frame labelled identity.

To summarize briefly, the poems offer readers a sense of intimacy, yet without 'characters': the narrating persons lack the dependable outlines expected of fictional characters. And this applies equally to any notion of a 'speaker' or author 'behind' the poem: we are given only evanescent fragments of personhood – which makes the atmosphere all the more pleasurable. This is different from the standard idea of a poem as the expression of feeling by a special individual, who is above ordinary humanity and speaks for them. Such an idea of poetry is derived from a narrow reading of Romanticism (Coleridge, Byron, Keats, Shelley) and was rejected by Modernist poets (Mallarmé, Eliot, Pound). Carol Ann Duffy expresses the standard position: 'Poets write about feelings, and we always fail.'[14] Writing 'about feelings' assumes that the role of the poet is to express the already existing social individual, and leaves no place for poetry that rebels against a society that packages identities for consumption.

There comes in reading Harwood the sheer pleasure of being in among things, 'the luxury of being alive', as he writes in 'For Paul [Evans]/ Coming out of winter': an absolute pleasure. That might seem to indicate that this is a poetry that turns its back on politics. But if the poetry does not seem to be immediately political, this is because politics has got split off from happiness: the mediations of politics, the language and images that characterize it, have got nothing to do with happiness. Happiness, moreover, is not entertainment: being entertained is perfectly compatible with unhappiness. In a society that consumes happiness rather than lives it, there is no time in which 'the luxury of being alive' can be experienced. But with the poems, time saturates their forms of expression: the microvariations of pulse and tempo that constitute aliveness.

Harwood's poems avoid giving us completed persons or completed feelings. A further technique of suspended completion begins in *The Sinking Colony* (1968–9): the use of typographical gaps which not only interrupt phrases but also sometimes cut them off in the middle, so that the word or words necessary to complete them grammatically are actually missing. This aspect of his poetry has generated some interesting critical discussion, as for instance in Robert Sheppard's useful essay, 'Lee Harwood and the Poetics of the Open Work'.[15] The poem 'Linen', already mentioned, offers some of the most vivid examples of such gaps:

>   touching you   like the
>   and soft as
>   like the scent of flowers and

(CP 144)

The strategy has to do with the type of reading Harwood wants to elicit, where the poem is

> a set of facts presented to you, the reader [...] and you, the reader take these facts, and the way the artist puts them together helps to influence the way you take them. But it must be facts, there must be no sloppiness or weakness or falling back on stylistics. You admit the complexity but you accept the responsibility.[16]

The responsibility, therefore, is mutual: 'the reader has to put into the poem as much as [the poet] put into it'.[17] Let it be said also that the engagement elicited from a reader does not entail her or him finding specific words to 'fill the gaps', or specific actions to fit the plot as in fantasy role-playing games, but a stronger responsibility. The breaks in rhythm bring in emotion, there's an emotion that's unresolved, and the reader has to handle multiple possibilities, and make distinctions. The engagement, in other words, is not designed to confirm the ego, the habitual self, which imagines itself as already complete.

The lines quoted above are not the only type of gap deployed by 'Linen'. It opens as follows:

> waking on the purple sheets whose softness
> The streets heavy with summer   the night thick with green leaves
> drifting into sleep we lay
> The dazzle of morning   the hot pavements
> fruit markets   'The Avenues'

The phrase ending in 'softness' would require several words to be completed. But this is not (or not necessarily) the case after 'summer', 'green leaves', 'we lay', 'morning', 'pavements', or 'markets': they can be read as complete phrases. Yet no grammatical relation is given between these particular phrases and the ones that follow them; narrative connections are not provided; we do not know what the relation is between the objects and events of one phrase and those of another; no overall scenario is given into which the details can be fitted. In the recording, Harwood leaves as long a gap after 'leaves', 'we lay', and 'markets', as he does after 'softness'. It seems therefore that the gaps relating to incomplete phrases belong to a larger set of gaps which occur between the objects, occasions, and speech-actions that when assembled together make up the poem. The incompleteness of phrases is lined up with the rhythm of the everyday, the durational present: the way in which it is cut up by discrete images. Harwood draws an analogy with film: 'if you look at people like Truffaut, Godard, and Resnais, you find this continual cross-cut collage effect – no plot, no beginning – middle – end routine'. He finds 'the same thing in painting: people like Larry Rivers' pictures with unfinished areas or with a figure half painted and arrows pointing, saying "nose" and "mouth"'. Once again, it is the idea of the audience engaged along with the artist in taking decisions. These make up the composition, which includes a shared and perhaps humorous recognition of clichés, of expectations about what is supposed to come next. But also, as with the paintings of Franz Kline, there can be a high degree of non-fixity of meaning: 'you have this area in black and white in a canvas and what you make of it is what the picture is – each person gets a different thing from the painting'. The use of gaps therefore can be taken as part of a broader strategy, which makes the poem open to various types of uncertainty. It is like Mallarmé's strategy: put the empty spaces that are normally around the edge of the poem into the poem.

The gaps between different types of speech-action are emphasized in 'Linen' by a switch to the language of comics and the scene-making techniques it uses:

> on the beaches
> machine-gunning the fleeing army
> the fighters coming in low 'at zero'
> the sun behind them   and bombs falling all round
> 'Jah Jah'   click click   'Jah Jah'

On the page of the comic (in this case a war comic, popular among boys in the fifties),[18] 'Jah Jah' would be words in bubbles and 'click click' the sound of triggers pulled, jaggedly hand-written across the frame, the words buzzing with immediacy as if actually happening, in a meeting between film and graphics. The poetics of the comic break through the boundaries that mark off conventional poetry. Comics were a powerful form of the wider post-war culture, and were kept out of 'literary' writing.

What then of an ordinary reader's actual encounter with these various types of gap and doubt, as opposed to what an academically trained reader has learned to do? Robert Sheppard has made the suggestion that readers may not in fact 'attempt the participation desired by Harwood';[19] in other words, that the technique may not work. In a survey designed to test readers' responses to this poem, Vesna Klein recorded a variety of different ways in which they had handled the gaps. One response seems to confirm Sheppard's point: 'It's missing pieces which seems a little obscure, are you meant to read into it? As to meaning, it is too vague to the point of making me wonder why bother.' While this reader recognized that the gaps can be taken as an invitation, another was baffled: 'I think I got a version that has been denied some key words!' A third reader, however, said: 'The unusual use of punctuation and gaps is so strong that [it] could stimulate even a deaf [person] to have an audible feeling about it!'[20] The survey was addressed to a sample of graduate students of the University of London; approximately half were literature students, and the rest were studying a variety of subjects, such as – in the case of the three responses quoted above – architecture, microbiology, and anthropology. Curiously, perhaps, the literature students were less bothered or surprised by the gaps ('literary background participants considered them as a sort of punctuation, and did not comment on them'), but by the same token their responses are less interesting. Presumably, having made the poem into a Literary object, they then went about completing it along the lines of their training. The respondents who really engaged with the gaps and were excited by the possibilities they generate did so because they got some pleasure from reading the poem. Overall, though, the majority of interviewees from both backgrounds did enter into becoming co-producers of the poem in one particular way: they 'sought a [...] narrative in order to make sense of the poem.'

But what type of narrative is needed in order to make the poems readable? 'Animal Days' is a poem made up of six sections that include a fairly large number of narrative fragments, some of which are as brief as a single line. The main way one makes sense of them is through placing the fragments in particular contexts. The first two lines ('The polo season would start early in April/ so there was no time to be wasted' (*CP* 149)) require a colonial context; the quoted statement tells of the thoughts of someone to whom the rhythms of colonial life are ordinary and everyday. They are taken from *The Last Englishman: The Autobiography of Lieut. Col. A. D. Wintle, M.C.*[21] Later fragments which mention 'rifles' and a 'mission' in the 'jungle' appear to belong to the same type of context.

A different context is conjured up by '"knights on horses"? "gentle ladies"? "towers in the forest"?' Here medieval chivalry would be the scenario, though the quoted phrases might belong to a nineteenth-century or Edwardian version of the Middle Ages. The question marks have been placed outside the quotation marks and therefore do not address someone who belongs inside the world told of but rather are directed to the outside that the reader of Harwood's poem inhabits, the reader who has to take decisions. Another narrative framework is summoned with the lines 'the Indian chiefs/ what are the wounds, anyway, and their cost?' (*CP* 150). Here the ordinary person's repertoire of narrative scenarios will come up with 'The West', yet the second line's moral ambiguities will probably cause a stereotyping reading to stumble. The colonial, the chivalric, the West are all inherited stories that continue to shape the present; Harwood brings them into play but also problematizes them. What sort of place do they put us in as we read them? What kind of history and what type of present do they offer? After all, there is no present as such, only the one that people are involved in composing. And that is the idea which Harwood has of the present of poetry, where 'a poem is [...] a common, shared object. And the object for me essentially must have loose ends, [...] because the reader or anyone else outside you has to complete it and make the final thing, if ever there is to be a final thing.'[22] This would also mean conceiving of history democratically, as the result of everybody's stories. As Michel de Certeau reminds us, history is a function of the present.[23]

But of course, it is not simply a question of 'people' and 'the present'. There are also the media through which what makes up present time has been formed: tv, film, print, radio. The juxtaposition of pieces of narrative in 'Animal Days' would be hard to imagine outside the film era. Yet Harwood's primary medium, though it is cut across by others, is print: he uses quote marks, direct and indirect speech, verbal stereotypes and morally ambiguous phrases, in order to open the act of reading to effects of visual media.

Unlike the poetry of simple nostalgia or of what Peter Middleton has called 'memoryism', the poem does not offer a reader a simple place to inhabit: one is pulled this way and that, by the interaction of different mediations and interpretations.[24] There is for example the pull of the heart, inside the vulnerable softness of the mammal body: 'holding a young rabbit in my hands/ walking across the stubble in the late afternoon' (*CP* 151) – another narrative fragment but one in which flesh is laid open to shock by the unformed present, the present which is not yet narrative and perhaps cannot become narrative or – consequently – history. The words do not allow the satisfaction of identity in knowing who 'we' are. In section 3, similarly, there is a moment when the known pattern of time, which history would be, dissolves into 'what approaches in the darkness// beyond all knowledge'. This is not that 'moment in the rose-garden', which T. S. Eliot's *Four Quartets* speaks of, where a mythical wholeness transcends history. Harwood's poem, by its composition, makes gaps in known historical scenarios by opening them to what is not known. There is no getting outside or above history, transcending it through a religious sense of a higher order of reality, as in Eliot or, earlier, Matthew Arnold; instead, there are narrative fragments, some biographical, some historical, and alongside them lapses of unformed time. These formed and unformed materials that alternate, although they will not fuse together in a single narrative, offer a consistency: the recurrent emergence and loss of pattern which is the texture of everyday life.

By offering not the perspective of a unique perceiver, but various entries into a field of relations, Harwood uses methods similar to those developed by American poets such as William Carlos Williams and Charles Olson.[25] The poem explores the contexts that produce subjectivity, or more accurately the contexts and media through which subjects are involved in producing present time. What it refuses to do is to make history into a single receding perspective that fits smoothly together and which 'we' can inherit as the ground of a common life. Harwood gives us scenes whose relationships do not resolve into single meaning. What is brought to attention, therefore, is a 'politics of subjectivity', to use Peter Middleton's phrase, and part of what the writing does, rather than to express 'the cultural identity of the author', is to investigate critically 'available public forms of linguistically produced subjectivity'.[26]

The date 1970 places the poem at the end of the decade of Prime Minister Macmillan's famous 'winds of change' speech, his reference to the inevitability of decolonization and the end of Empire. The book that 'Animal Days' appeared in, *The Sinking Colony*, neatly names the crisis of colonial memory and of a version of Englishness related to Empire. In this sense, along with a number of other Harwood poems of that time, it traces the stories and images available to a young person living in the UK in the 1960s. The scenes overlap, collide, bleed into each other; they have not been pressed into the coherence of a historical 'us' for readers to identify with.

Harwood's poetry did not conform to the reactive and restrictive version of poetic language that poets of the Movement, such as Philip Larkin, had made it their business to justify. With its self-deprecating and self-defensive irony, Movement poetry offered readers a haven from change. Its language excluded the incomplete, the formless and the unpredictable. The taste that informs Movement poetry can be traced back to Matthew Arnold and his rejection, for example, of Keats and Shelley for being 'on a false track' when 'they set themselves to reproduce the exuberance of expression ... the richness of images ... of the Elizabethan poets'.[27] Arnold's famous 1851 poem 'Dover Beach' brings his idea of serious language to the abyss that he felt threatened the global destiny that most Victorians took to be an Englishman's birthright. The poet listens to the noise of the surf at night, but instead of 'the Sea of Faith' which used to encircle the earth, 'like the folds of a bright girdle', he hears only 'its melancholy, long, withdrawing roar,/ Retreating [...]/ down [...] the vast edges drear/ And naked shingles of the world'.[28] What has been lost? If religion is the solution from which crystallize the forms that permit 'unity of being',[29] by uniting self and world, 'faith' can at the same time be read as the collection of beliefs, in other words fantasies, that gave coherence to the British Empire. Remove them, and instead of 'the world, which seems/ To lie before us like a land of dreams', what remain are only the 'confused alarms of struggle and flight,/ Where ignorant armies clash by night'. The metaphoric language, pledge of the timeless ('bright girdle'), has ceased and become instead a nostalgic space haunted by absence: a premonition of the twentieth century perhaps, but certainly an understanding of how far the power of those 'dreams' was underwritten by a world order.

The continuity between inner life and public space, which Arnold mourned but in mourning held onto, was finished as far as Lee Harwood's generation were concerned. In the hundred or so years between them, the work of Yeats, Eliot, Auden, and others traced the many chasms between lyrical poetry and public discourse that would lead Harwood and other late Modernist poets to rethink the lyric. In particular, the notion of the lyric as the expression of a unified and representative self was no longer viable for them. Harwood's early poem 'Cable Street' includes the lyric voice as only one item in a collection of materials that have no single order. The poem declares itself a response to suggestions 'that I should write about Brick Lane and Cable Street, two areas that I know intimately, having lived in the same these last six years' (*CP* 16),[30] yet it does not base itself on an autobiographical narrative or other form of personal testimony. Auden's poetry of the 1930s, such as 'A Bride in the 30s', 'Dover', or 'In Memory of W. B. Yeats', had used diverse types of language, yet there was always a bridge between the personal and the public through the use of a unified tone for all the materials. 'Cable Street' has no such overall tone: there's a typewritten letter from the Ministry of Housing about a compulsory purchase order which mentions 'general rehousing' and then adds in the final sentence, 'I would mention, however, that it might be some twelve to eighteen months or more before the Council would be in a position to begin general rehousing' (*CP* 17). The civil service prose exploits the communicative pact of postwar public consensus – the recipient is supposed to be in a civilized conversation with the sender – to tell you you'll be homeless for up to eighteen months. The tone of the letter is also irreconcilable with the various lyrical fragments, which are themselves interspersed with prose passages. Not only is there no single genre to hold the poem together, it breaks the 'rules' – i.e the expectations that govern and regulate both public discourse and literature.

The opening four-line lyrical fragment addresses a 'you'; to read it is to be drawn into intimacy with the Other but then repelled:

> blood
> dripping slowly
> from your throat.
>
> how can I watch you anymore.

Had Harwood written 'how can I watch *this*', there would not be a problem; the poem would have withdrawn from intimacy with the injured person to intimacy with the reader ('hypocrite reader', as Baudelaire wrote). The repulsion is not just physical (the blood) but communicative: the intimate 'you' continues to be the person whose throat is dripping blood but the act of addressing them becomes impossible. This is not supposed to happen: it breaks the rules of communication: there is an 'I' and a 'you' but no 'we'. The hypocrite reader is apt to rush in, trying to restore the world of shared experience, but this is not possible. The impossibility hinges on violence cutting into the other's body, without motive – a not unusual scene when the film and literature of the 1970s began to make motiveless violence commonplace, an exposure of the incoherence of actual societies.

Other lyric passages address a 'you', revealed to be a lover:

> the moon so clear in the sky
> above these city trees
> your lips and eyes
> so tender filled with love.
>
> (CP 17)

Yet although a reader can share in the intimacy, there is no common ground between the experience of the lovers and drug dealers of the present and the hunger marchers and anti-fascist marchers of the past who are part of the poem's East End scenario. Auden or the Movement poets would have looked to irony so as to contain all of the materials presented within the author's tone of voice. When Philip Larkin's famous poem 'High Windows' registers the rejection, by a younger generation, of the 'bonds and gestures' of traditional imagined community, it responds with an image of complete emptiness: 'rather than words comes the thought of high windows:/ The sun-comprehending glass,/ And beyond it, the deep blue air, that shows/ Nothing, and is nowhere, and is endless'. Here as irony reaches its limit so also does conservative poetic form: it can register unbridled desire only as the emptying of traditional forms (the 'high windows' suggest Church or School).[31]

'High Windows' responds to a split society with a desire for homogeneous, empty space. 'Cable Street', on the other hand, embraces heterogeneity; there is only the incoherence of the actual, without any overarching principle or common discourse, which people have been led to expect the state – or poetry – to provide. There seems no doubt that this lack of a unifying language is a significant part of the reason why the mainstream poetry institutions decided that this type of poem was not poetry: it did not offer a common language.

Instead, there are a variety of types of language, making different scenarios (science fiction, voices of Lenin and Churchill, a children's story, Émile Zola, quantum physics, racism, etc.), without coherence except that they demand the ability to comprehend their relationships. There is no overarching narrative to bind them together, but the way the poem places different forms of social life beside each other speaks of a commonality that might be realized in a future society.

The conservative mainstream of British poetry of the past fifty years has relied upon a consensual 'we' to establish its communicative action.[32] Conservative poems can be outrageous in their references (e.g. to sex, violence, drugs) without breaking with the consensual 'we'. That this communicative stance might be complicitous with ongoing class division, does not enter the equation.[33] A reader looking for a 'community' that overrides social antagonism, or even a 'multicultural' society of different groups who nevertheless speak to each other (the East Enders model) will not find that here. 'Cable Street' is composed of lyrical and narrative fragments placed together with 'found' materials, i.e. unprocessed data brought into the poem.

The Long Black Veil, a longer poem of some thirty pages that Harwood wrote in the early 1970s, grapples with the difficulty of how to bring the complexity of lived experience across into writing. The poem is divided into twelve 'books' and is subtitled *A Notebook 1970–72*; the theme alluded to in the title, taken from a Country song about adultery, is a relationship with a married woman. Formally it is more ambitious than the earlier long poem; a crucial difference is that the collage method of 'Cable Street' is complicated by the added technique of montage; as

Robert Sheppard notes, quoting Harwood's description of his approach: 'one actuality in time set (beside) another, causing waves to go between the two', an idea which 'echoes Eisenstein's theory of montage which regards the combination of discrete shots not as a simple sequence, but as the creation of a new conceptual unit'.[34] One of the poem's epigraphs, a quotation from Ezra Pound, speaks of 'comprehension of process', i.e. of the understanding of change in time, which allows temporality, as Sheppard puts it, 'to expand beyond the single instant'. The form of the writing varies as it tracks the different shapes, rhythms, times, and places of the materials of experience (e.g. prose journal entries, letters, passages from Rilke and Gide, a page with only four lines surrounded by blank space). Decisions about form, therefore, arise out of a need to comprehend experience in its particularity and variousness; the existential process and the writing process cross over into each other: instead of the lyric as a transcendent instant of time, *The Long Black Veil* presents its own writing as a shaping movement that occurs over a period of time (two years).

As an alternative to placing the materials in a linear narrative sequence, Harwood opts for what he calls 'a mosaic structure [...] pioneered in this century by people like James Joyce and Ezra Pound. It is the concept of relativity'.[35] This implies multiple rather than simple relationships between the different movements of the poem; rather than a linear development, a 'drift':

>How to accept
>this drift
>
>the move   not mapped
>nor clear other than in
>its existence

(CP 168)

A map implies an act of representation, whose formula can be repeated over the whole area to be included; in terms of writing, a language that can classify and lay a grid over experience. Here the nature of the challenge the poem sets itself: not to rigidify and simplify, even though those types of controlling pattern might diminish anxieties of uncertainty ('How do we live with this?' the poem asks). The words 'drift' and 'move' do not offer the kind of handle on time that definitions would provide. Definitions have to fulfil the condition of being clearer than that which they define; they are also necessarily nouns or noun phrases; in other words, they have to function as names. There is a connection here with a story mentioned at the end of the 'Preface', 'the Sufi story of the famous River that tried to cross the desert, but only crossed the sands as water "in the arms of the wind", nameless but' (*CP* 169). The River had to become nameless in order to move across space and through time. The purchase of nouns upon the real gets loosened. How then to write?

The poem mixes prose passages with the more condensed language of poetry, while also moving between journal entries and fictions (or 'imaginings') which explore other ways of seeing. Thus, from Book 3:

> Go up to the wild strawberry patch again, squat down and eat some. Continue up along the road, the pine woods by the crest of the ridge 'see for miles'
>
> You walk through the door
> No, now you stop your car in a small town square
> I get up from the porch step and greet you
> This is all 'country manners'
>
> There's no steamer bringing you to me
> up-river at the hill-station
> No long white dress on the verandah
>
> It is ...
> I hold you.   Isn't this enough?
>
> <div align="right">(<i>CP</i> 173)</div>

Each of the four groups of lines is a different way of writing, and each does different things. The first, printed as prose, has the quality of a diary, choosing detail without clear emergence of shape, until its third line moves into precisely that, the view clarified – and this is the place or moment where the typography changes to signal 'poetry'. The concern with how to shift from one degree of detail to another and from randomness to pattern, from random encounter to formal relation, continues through into the second section. Interestingly, the poem rejects the first statement ('you walk through the door') for something more adequate. More adequate to what though? Certainly not to 'the way it was', since the past – in this poem – is not a simple thing that can be laid hold of once and for all. 'Country manners' are somewhere between habit and ritual, which are degrees of formalization of living; once again the poem shows a fascination with the interstitial space between the random and the formal ('the fascination with *this* formality, *this* ritual'), as these cross back and forth between writing and life. Thus form in this poem does not obey socially shaped habits of memory – the past filtered to suit the narratives of the present – on the contrary, it searches out ways of displaying and changing those filters. Thus the writing, in an important sense, is not 'after the event' but part of discovering what actually makes it an event: not an ideal event to be found when all the filters are removed but one that exists where different ways of seeing intersect, where the relation between them can be grasped.

The third group of lines quoted above is a 'fiction', a romantic genre of fiction marked by certain stereotypic nouns: 'steamer', 'hill-station', 'verandah', all of which carry the atmosphere of a British colony (verandah is a borrowed Hindi word). The 'long white dress' is a different type of stereotype, less limited historically or geographically; possibly it is related to the song of the title, but perhaps it is not a stereotype at all but an image of love. The difficulty of knowing is part of what the poem is about. The 'nos' ('no steamer', 'no long white dress') give a strong charge to the affirmative 'It is ... ' that follows, as if here, finally, the real authentic expression of the relationship will be given. But the 'it' is left hanging without definition; no noun comes to express it. Instead, there is an action: 'I hold you'; instead of a (clear) scene that can be named and described, an action that has not yet become an event. As a form of statement, 'It is ... ' leads us to expect a world made up of people and objects. Instead, we get a possibility which may become an event. The problem is not just nouns and the fixity they tend to presuppose, but the game of equivalences that 'is' statements wrap us in: *The Long Black Veil* takes us into a profound shake-up of language. The subject of the 'it' that has been left hanging could be the two preceding scenes, or the love affair, or the poem itself, or the relation between writing and the real – or all of those at once. And yet, nouns (and noun clauses) make up a good proportion of the poem, especially the prose-journal parts: the problem is posed, not necessarily resolved.

The transition from randomness to pattern, from the formless to experience, involves not isolating a local meaning but generating a shifting field of relations between heterogeneous materials: a larger-scale question than Harwood's earlier concern with how framing affects a scene of a poem, and more complex than the problems posed in 'Cable Street'. The larger question can only be worked at in a poem which is longer than the ones he had previously written. Yet within this complexity, he is also concerned with simplicity, with 'talking straight', as he puts it. He had realized

> that it is possible to write directly, in a personal way, but – a big but – that it must be straight. You must be talking straight, and it must be set in contexts: in contexts of time, and contexts of place. And so, personal writing was no longer whimpering, but was like, I use the word, tough, but not with any Ted Hughes references, but it must be tough thinking.[36]

Here is an example of directness from the 'Preface', where the reference is to separation and the 'year' which has 'passed':

> How do we live with this?
> yet live with this

(*CP* 168)

Directness is not to be confused with having answers, with having labels for things. The 'yet' in the second line modifies the question, to how to stay with the real and not move into a detemporalizing discourse, not close it – since the question could imply the kind of answer that names experience in order to fix and contain it; two lines further on there is a quote from Joanne Kyger: 'Concepts promise protection/ from experience.'

Experience includes time: the question of how to include time in writing – as a function of the verbal materials themselves rather than as an idea represented, so that the poem itself becomes something that occurs – is a key concern of Anglo-American poetics of the 1960s and after. Lee Harwood's approach is in this respect similar to Robert Creeley's in the seminal book *Pieces* (1969).[37] More simply, there is a Zen-like quality to the phrase 'yet live with this', an instigation to move from the verbal real to the actual real or, more accurately, to find how the two occupy the same space.

The effect of varying 'contexts of time [...] and space' that Harwood refers to, also involves the various positions from which communicative actions can be undertaken. When a reader comes to

> My heart weeps
>
> Who would ever have thought I'd write that?
> 'My heart weeps'?
>
> (*CP* 182)

s/he is given the statement twice, the second time with quotation marks. Quotation marks signal another speaker or writer. But in this case, who is this other, who is the person who might have written that? It is actually more a *where* question, where could that have been written from? To attempt an answer would involve working out what type of literature (e.g. melodrama perhaps?), in what period (Victorian, Edwardian?), and with what rhetorical characteristics (possibly a discourse which levels speaker and hearer to a common humanity?). As a question about language, it is highly complex. Yet there is also a gain in meaning: to think of a phrase as coming from somewhere else and yet still use it, is to find the image of an emotion within it, as another time and place become momentarily fused with the present.

Book 6 begins with a statement, 'The questions of complexity' (*CP* 177), that refers both to a way of thinking about a relationship and to the writing of the poem itself. At one level, 'complexity' connects with an essay on marriage by Jung, first published in 1925, in which he argues that the more complex personality in a couple will tend to contain the simpler one; the advantage for the 'contained' is that they will be 'undivided', and the disadvantage that they will tend to depend on the other.[38] The poem uses the ideas of container and contained in order to think about love as interplay of closeness and distance: 'somehow to have all one's hopes there,/ to see and touch, to be wholly in one place./ Yet over the horizon   as real as any ... ' (*CP* 178) The ideas also work to hold within thought the opposing notions of conscious and unconscious or female and male without fixing them in a grid of binaries; 'one within the other/ a continual shifting   and that both ways/ – more a flow – from the simplicity to the complexity'.

The poem itself shifts between container and contained. It takes the poetics of 'Cable Street' further by including passages that probe its own ways of cohering as a poem. That includes the relation between language and the real and extends into an ethics of writing that stresses 'The falsity when anything becomes a symbol' (*CP* 179). There is a decision for immanence as a way of thinking, as opposed to seeking solutions in transcendence: 'No godhead, no gospel, but a "multiplicity of approaches", each in its own right, each immanent in nature' (*CP* 181). The same principle of discovering forms of understanding which are immanent to nature itself can be found in any number of Renaissance thinkers, such as Bacon with his famous principle of removing all 'idols' from thought. Thus the poem engages with a longer time span and relives the bases of modern thought – the last passage quoted ('No godhead ... ') comes after a page or so about Egyptian statuary seen in a Boston museum, recounting with some fascination the symbolic powers of Egyptian gods. The concern is to retrieve the powers of the intellect from capture by its own products, which are not only gods and symbols but all theories, concepts, and schemas which reduce the material of experience. In particular, the poem restores the shaping power of intellect in love, instead of opting for the standard opposition of emotion and intellect. But where, for Jung, the work of intellect permits to the other in a relationship the undividedness of 'being contained spiritually', for Harwood intellect is 'the container *and* the contained', continually changing places, both in the relationship and in thought, without hierarchy. He does not uphold undividedness or 'spiritual wholeness' (to give it its usual name) as an ideal; instead, morally *and* formally, he proposes actual multiplicities.

The Long Black Veil is unmistakably contemporary in its way of thinking. In his essay on the twentieth century, the American historian Henry Adams puts the alchemical idea of the universal solvent (figured, for example, in Mercury as god and metal that dissolves gold) together with the scientific idea of phase as a state of matter (as in solid, liquid, and gas), and plays with the notion of phase-change as a way of talking about epochal shifts in history. For Adams, entry into the twentieth century, with its unprecedented acceleration of change, is marked by a phase-change in which the solvent has dematerialized and become thought itself. At the moment of phase-change there is uncertainty or 'drift', to use Harwood's word, between one state of matter and another, when you cannot know which way the particles are moving. *The Long Black Veil* grapples with change as historical and psychic at the same time, and with love as inner and outer fact. Its 'universal solvent' is imagination:

> I will call anything that goes on in my head 'a dream', whether it be thoughts or imaginings, daydreams or sleep dreams. They all give pictures of 'the possible', and that is exactly their value.
>
> (*CP* 172)

Thus imagination produces the possible, and the possible is what becomes person, thing, event. Stated more classically, by Kant, the imagination apprehends phenomena previous to their understanding. Harwood combines this Romantic notion of imagination with a postmodern sense of experience as a complex intersection of fictions.

Intelligence which obviates the need for God or symbolic surrogates is, at base, the power of thought to alter itself. For the French poet Mallarmé, at the beginnings of Modernism, it is embodied in the book, or poem-book; in this sense too, *The Long Black Veil* recuperates the sources of an inheritance. The intellect is what holds materials together in a field, it is what makes the field, and is not to be confused with thought in its bureaucratic or managerial forms (the 'monster [which] haunts us – continually aroused at/ each "wrong" word, each "wrong" action' (*CP* 183)). In Modernist poetics, it is complexity at the level of formal composition, causing 'waves to go between' one actuality and another, as Harwood says of Joyce's *Ulysses*, once again going to the source: 'you have different people doing different things within one city, all equally important, and all somehow relating in a mysterious way. The bridges, which aren't pointed out with a big line A to B to C, are the real magic in his work. I mean magic in the real sense of power.'[39]

Book 8 of *The Long Black Veil* holds a mirror to the process of composition by showing the reader some of the decisions that confronted the writer. First there is the difficulty of finding a language for emotion: 'My heart weeps' (*CP* 182). The statement moves between intimacy and strangeness, directness and indirectness, as the poem grapples with the difficulty that emotion is both immediate, a pulsation of the body, and mediated by social languages at a given time and place: thus finding a language of the self which is not in some way estranging might be impossible. If the immediate is always discursively mediated, there is no pure voice of the self, another voice will always come in, and direct lyrical simplicity will always be complex, multiple. The passage that follows consists of a quotation from Paul Valéry that speaks of the need to avoid the facile ('You must try, Psyche, to use up all your facility against an obstacle; face the granite, rouse yourself against it, and for a while despair.') Next there is a reply to Valéry; instead of the figure of a sculptor in front of the intractable stone, a different idea of difficulty is proposed: 'Not a climbing, but a moving across the surface in a certain way, as though a soaking into the grain, what was there all the time, though never fully realized.' What the writer struggles with in this case would be how to find a way of writing that touches the fine grain of reality and does not simply make images that cover it over. There follows a scene of writing that has already been mentioned: it is the nightmarish 'monster' which demands that all the words be right – an obsession with correctness which would, like Blake's Urizen, trap the intellect in rigid schemes of reason. Finally, there is a brief quotation from the modern German poet Rilke: 'Each single angel is terrifying.' In Rilke's book, the *Duino Elegies,* the Angel is, as in Sufi angelology, the figure of the self-sufficient ecstatic intellect, which makes the ordinary self redundant, through a presencing of the wholly Other. The various ways in which intellect works – and can get trapped – are displayed in all these figurations of the process of writing. Their interaction is not linear but like a moving mosaic: they expose the shifting surfaces of meaning.

This chapter has sought to offer not a survey of the whole of Harwood's poetry but a view of its constituting principles as a lifetime's work. Some of the possibilities opened up by the exploratory writing of *The Long Black Veil* can only fully be appreciated by reading the later books. One of the things that he tends to do after the mid 1970s is to redistribute the long poem; the compositional features of *The Long Black Veil* are now to be found spread throughout the various poems that make up a book. In this final part of the chapter, the aim is to indicate what the poems are capable of doing, about which there is perhaps less to be said and more to be experienced. Certainly, it is harder to say what the poems can do than to offer an account of their composition.

Poets of the parallel tradition, instead of relying on traditional forms of narrative and lyric, were exploring different ways of placing materials in a poem. Open field poetry is a common name for this approach to composition.[40] Its artistic genealogy goes back to the widespread use of collage by early Modernist writers as well as painters. Yet the terms 'collage' or 'open field' do not of themselves describe the actual relationships between the materials that make up the poem. 'Magic' and 'grain' are words that Harwood has used to speak about attention to local detail, and both imply that the patterns should emerge, as the emotion does, rather than being imposed by any type of schematics. In *The Long Black Veil* he puts the relationships between the materials flush with the relationship of the lovers, just as Basil Bunting, in his poem 'Villon', traces failure of poetic composition to a failure in love. The poem 'Qasida', from Harwood's book *Qasida Island* (written between 1971 and 1972), starts with a series of phrases that repeatedly bring the reader back to a beginning:

> it's *that*
> the quiet room
> the window open, trees outside
> 'blowing' in the wind.
> the colour is called green.
> the sky.
> the colour is called blue.
> (sigh)   the crickets singing

(CP 196)

There are five opening *the*s and in addition the 'it's *that*' of the first line: all constitute a *pointing* action. Yet what they indicate is not given as a whole scene: there are only successive moments or 'waves' that do not add up to a framed scenario. Words like 'that' and 'the' have been disembedded from discourse and from transparency, and used to point up temporary surfaces. We are given the gesture of reference but not its fulfilment in a scene we can inhabit.

From the fourth line of the passage quoted ('"blowing" in the wind') to the end of it, the writing begins to draw attention to language as a labelling action, at first gently, through 'blowing' with the quotation marks around it, and then more emphatically with the three repeated *the*s and with the references to naming ('is called'). What really breaks the lure of resting in language as if it were nature is '(sigh)', because of the particular way it makes the word visible and tangible, as in a comic, where sounds which are not words are put inside balloons, just as the reference-function of language starts to relate not to things but to the naming of things ('the colour is called green' refers to referring itself). The Word's tangibility and visibility become its prime effect, a surface to be enjoyed for its own sake.

Half a page or so later, it's the physicality of words that comes foremost:

> the words come slowly. No ...
> your tongue   the lips moving
> the words reach out –
> crude symbols – the hieroglyphs
> sounds, *not* pictures
>
> the touching beyond this –
> I touch you

(*CP* 196–7)

The poem has moved from reference to words as physical, coming off the tongue, their materiality in their sound; to take hieroglyphs to be 'pictures' would be to eliminate that bodily materiality. The subject has become the tangibility of words, where touching implies a body with thickness, with carnal density; words anticipate contact with flesh. But then there is something 'beyond' this fact of language and the words that tell of it. There's a silence that permits something else to come: the familiar act of touching becomes something strange, as though experienced for the first time. By drawing attention to words as labels, the poem makes tangible the prison-house of language, as Nietzsche called it.[41] In turn, in a second wave, what is outside words becomes tangible ('the touching beyond this'). The writing brings that also into language, but a different language, language altered by the poem, by the poem's silence.

There is a sense, then, in which fully to give oneself to

reading a Harwood poem means to loosen the hold of interpretation which, by always having something to say, clutters the apprehension of the silences, the empty spaces and times the poem acknowledges. These poems move against the crushing of attention by a culture that plugs consciousness into constant streams of information, that is, reins people into consuming information through the lure of recognition that gives security of possession. The terrain of the poem is where flesh and uncertainty meet. Take the following:

> windows open. You move ...
> No, not so much a moving
> but the artificiality of containment
> in one skin. 'No man an island' (ha-ha Buddha)
> ... lonesome, huh?

Quietly the whole territory shifts: from 'you move' to *what moves and what is moves*. Instead of developing a *theme* by answering 'not so much a moving' with a phrase of the same order like 'as a drifting', the poem pulls the rug from under the universe of comparisons, and plunges the act of reading into a terrain where the physical individual does not rule.

Where there's that degree of uncertainty and unfamiliarity, philosophy and religion tend to rush in. But even the silence of the Buddha fails to lure the poem into resolution. Instead, it stays outside, with laughter. There is a Zen touch to this, as there is to

> when the wind gets cold
> we'll put our sweaters on
> it's that simple, really ...
>
> (CP 197)

The statements about language, the folding of language onto itself, here fall away into a stillness.

If that can happen, then poetry is neither a lens through which objects are made to appear nor itself an object to be thought about, but an opening onto the infinite inside experience. As Harwood writes,

> This is not about writing,
> but the whole process
> You step off the porch into the dry field
> You're there

> You see, you're *there*
> Now, take it from there ...
>
> (*CP* 198)

Once again a Zen feel comes into the language. The word *there* goes through a strange metamorphosis, which is difficult to describe conceptually, since as it repeats it dissolves the regime of reference, and thence of concepts, into a silence which permits hearing the word to become an incomparable 'thisness' – a beginning of everything, as the final phrase suggests. 'Take it from there' is also a phrase sometimes used by a jazz soloist when handing over to another, the poem here handing over its work to another.

That movement whereby language about language arises and then falls away is one of the later poems' constant characteristics, though rarely as explicitly as in 'Qasida'. One such case is 'Gorgeous – Yet Another Brighton Poem', which first uses the word *gorgeous*, then quotes its dictionary definition. With the placing of the definition at the end, followed by 'That's right' (*CP* 450), the act of definition or description becomes reabsorbed into the lovely surfaces that make up the poem. This was always the case with Harwood's poetry, as with that notion of bringing out the grain that was already there in the material, but the later poems are touched by a deepening stillness ('as though all my life I've been approaching/ this' (*CP* 134)):

> To fall in love with the countryside
> and stay in that love
> writing love poems
>
> in one's head, one's eyes, one's fingers,
> one's body   walking
> through the hot July wheatfields
> heady with the scent of camomile.
>
> Poems beyond any words
> of explanation

The earlier work had avoided giving authority to any author figure by presenting all scenarios as fictions; the method now turns on placing language at the disposal of all the senses of a body no longer owned ('I never *am*; I am *becoming*').[42] The result is writing which borders on the terrain of mysticism, as suggested in the title of his 1998 book *Morning Light*, a phrase which connotes the dawn light of visionary experience, yet without any phantasmagoria of 'spiritual' presences:

> There are no ghosts here
> but as though we lived forever,
> all of history and ourselves alive in this one moment
> in one place with no wish to be elsewhere.
>
> (CP 314)

As Harwood writes in a letter, 'language is shot through with failures, but it's all we have'.[43] The type of attention he gives to it – both to language and to the (English) language – is not merely open to the mysterious and the strange, it is also streetwise. His writing acknowledges the quick turnover of expressions and the making and unmaking of cultural worlds in the context of urban survival, including the struggle for power which goes on inside language, with its changing historical and geopolitical dimensions. His book *All the Wrong Notes*, published in 1981, includes the complication of Victorian literature by the beginnings of US geopolitical power with the 1853 occupation of Okinawa; the way two frontiers, the US one and the Argentinian one, had in 1900 disappeared from the country and re-emerged in the city; and the 'Grand Events' of the 'dangerous times' of the French Resistance and British trade-unionism. All these are questions of history, or of how one reads – that is, the relationships of language with those events – and the suggestion is made that insofar as reading becomes active as part of writing, there can be no 'correct' expressions, in other words no 'right' correlation between history and language. Thus the book's title is drawn from a marginal note the American composer Charles Ives wrote on his manuscript score for *The Fourth of July*, in order to prevent the copyist from correcting it: 'All the wrong notes are right.'

Thus also, as the poem 'Bath-time' (CP 303) suggests, attempts to regulate and take possession of the language are incompatible with writing poetry. The poem registers 'chained numbness' as the public state of mind, and finds its index of the times in 'Cambridge Marxists', an expression that Barry MacSweeney, to whom the poem is dedicated, was later to use in a similar way ('Marxist Cambridge prefects, self-appointed/ guarantors of consonants and vowels/ and arrangement of everyday sentences').[44] Harwood adds,

'I don't need patronage I need something else': both poets equate Thatcherist times with an increased use of language as control.

Harwood finds in Chris Torrance an alternative guarantor of language:

> 'O ma blessure' groan the trees
> with the wounds of a multitude of small boys' penknives.
>
> No, not that –
> but the land, the musics, the books
> always attendant
> amongst the foolish rush and a scramble for vainglory,
> talk or noise for its own sake, a semblance of energy
> but not necessity.
>
> Throw your cap in the air, get on your bike, and pedal off
> down hill – it's a joy with no need of chatter,
> Hello Chris.
>
> (CP 299–300)

Torrance's exuberance, as we will see in the next chapter, is necessary precisely because it is useless. Harwood, similarly, asks: 'to finally pull the plug on the word machine,/ to rise from the chair late one evening/ and step back into the quiet and darkness?' (*CP* 299). His poetry, as this 'poem for writers' makes clear, embraces uncertainty, incompleteness and the outside which is not known – qualities that are useless when competing in 'the marketplace', that fetish of current English. There never was any verbal fetishism in Harwood's writing. And instead of locking with the language of power in passionate struggle, like MacSweeney's, Harwood's poems explore the limits of knowledge around whatever is, and the beginning of something else.

2

Chris Torrance:
Lyric and the Larger Process

> The outside invades and doubles over us.
>
> (Robin Blaser)

> A poet is a time mechanic not an embalmer.
>
> (Jack Spicer)

Chris Torrance was born in 1941 and grew up in the outer suburbs of south London. After working as a solicitor's clerk, he became a park gardener, first in London and then in Bristol. His physical trajectory from south London to Bristol, and then to the Upper Neath Valley in mid Wales has also been a spiritual and poetic journey, in which the self in isolation travels through phases of landscape, history and the cosmos that are received into that self from the outside and transform it. This depends upon an openness to whatever the outside may bring: too much filtering may block the process. The early 'Carshalton Poems', which track the beginnings of his relationship with poetry, start with an abandonment of predictable patterns of experience:

> That the affairs of man be planned
> by gods I do not, I do
> not
>   accept.
> unplanned,
>   unprofitable
>
> (*GOPR* 7)

This first section is a preface or preparation for self-creation, by a declaration of freedom and in particular freedom from gods,

gods that would include any conventional idea of Literature as access to status and permission to be a poet. He will not become a poet by using recognizable, conservative language. The freedom he embraces needs other forms and energies, as is made clear in an interview given in 1977, when he answers the question, 'How did you bring yourself to poetry?':

> what really took me out was meeting up with a fairly anarchic bunch of literary hooligans in the back bar of the Greyhound, Carshalton in the early '60s. We decided to pool our efforts and money and start a little mag which we called ORIGINS-DIVERSIONS. [...] There was a surge of 'underground poetry' from various sources as the influence of Ginsberg and the other beats became felt, and in the context of the burgeoning influence of CND. [...] A most important contact was with Lee Harwood, who was living in the East End at the time [...] He always had new books to show me [...] and in that way he spread a lot of influence in my direction [...] Lee's pourings into my consciousness were perhaps of the continental, surreal influence.[1]

He goes on to mention two other vital resources: the book *The New American Poetry 1945–1960*, which he 'bought merely because I recognised the names Kerouac, Ginsberg, Corso, Snyder, Ferlinghetti in it', and the young British poets committed to 'open field poetics' whom he came across through the magazine *The English Intelligencer*, run by Andrew Crozier and Jeremy Prynne.

The poet's location, in the 'Carshalton Poems', is the 'placid vacuous suburb', with its 'monotonous song' (*GOPR* 8). Yet the emptiness is not a lament for lost meaning (as in Betjeman or Larkin). It's a threshold of alteration ('alone & beside hysteria/ but quiet' (*GOPR* 7)) by other scenes, other musics:

> forms
> changed magicked alchemicked
> shimmering light
> no grasping it
> nothing special
> at all.

(*GOPR* 16)

That decision, to be open to unpredictable change, is followed through by the writing: we are not offered an autobiographical story or a received literary genre; the form has to follow from the decision, the decision creates the form, and the decision is to be open to the random (hence 'nothing special'). So poetry is not a question of looking for a pattern, a repeatable form, a guarantee ('gods' would be that), but of how, without that machinery, the self is buffeted by weather, by pain, attracted by suicide, subject to unpredictable refashioning by love. Colours and objects (for example a milk bottle top, grass, milk, sky) carry with them that 'edge of pain' and enter the field of vision the more sharply. It is among other things the pain of no change, of having lived in one place too long ('the same river/ floats under the same/ laconic stone bridge'). But at the edge, something else beckons and induces a type of trance: 'a red rust moon/ on a purple sky/ I must've been/ watching the/ 2 bats flying/ an hour or more (black/ rags') (*GOPR* 13).

In this book, surfeit is the thrust of whatever breaks the bounds of a repetitive and restricted life: 'I grow drunk on the scent of yellow wallflowers/ I am sunk in the heart of my love' (*GOPR* 22). And in the part is shown the whole: the poetry is in the surfeit, not in thought: 'thought/ is wasted/ on the green hill/ white & blue sky/ uncurling summer's promise' (*GOPR* 18). Yet 'Thought/ is wasted' can be read as a double meaning: a waste to think about the green hill, etc. (because thought would select and subordinate ...); but also thinking the hill, the sky, and the summer turns thinking into a wild energy that destroys itself, an expenditure. The first meaning of 'waste' is framed as 'the world's troubles/ [which] grind unceasingly on one thousand/ yards away from me/ on every side': the factory that produces continuity, the continuity of joyless utilitarian life. The other meaning is declared, in a subsequent poem, with the Blakean phrase: 'energy is paradise' (*GOPR* 29).[2] 'Thought' is both of these things. Lee Harwood, on the back cover of *Green Orange Purple Red*, writes, 'This experience, the poems, just makes you go "Wow!" and hurry off into the outside world looking from side to side and trying to take every detail in of the whole limitless visual experience waiting there.'

The sky, in these poems, is a place of ceaselessly changing forms: 'this morning/ you should have seen/ the sky, new/ forms every second' (*GOPR* 12). Thus Torrance's sky-gazing, a feature of all his books, places the poems at an edge between recognition and randomness, where patterns emerge and are also lost: they cannot be held still or possessed. The sense of ceaseless change extends from the outside into the inner life: 'The colours of blossoms, the swirling whiteness of fine weather clouds on warm days, nights cloistered with sky trails, lines, lives, emotions intersecting, intertwining, coloured by the dancing memory' (*GOPR* 9). The play of colours upon the visual imagination is continuous ('crimson lines', 'green gasometer', 'saffron rust', 'crimson night', and so on (*GOPR* 9, 11)); colours repeat through the book, but in different orders and juxtapositions: they do not make a fixed composition any more than 'the sky full of scurrying figures' does (*GOPR* 9). Alongside this mobile collage of colours and shapes, the poems give us a narrative –

> the herringbone sky
> six miles up
> passers-by frown as they edge by
> me sitting neck-
> stretched head up-
> craned on my grudging rollsroycesilvercloud
> jet-propelled super rotary cutter

(*GOPR* 12–13)

– where the reference is to Torrance's job as a council gardener. The humour abandons self-importance and self-dramatization, just as the tranced gaze abandons itself to 'nothing special/ at all'. To choose to be 'on the smooth plains of everyday', a space without idols – without mythology – means that 'there may be no excuses/ only this moment, now, the/ miracle/ of everyday' (*GOPR* 15). This, then, is the poet's permit.

The narrative of self includes love, but once again as the unpredictable: 'yr flesh & soul & the/ kindness of yr passion// driving me/ in strange directions, you,/ woman, creating calm in zones/ and driving daggers into parts' (*GOPR* 15). Love, which redistributes affect through the body, makes a strangeness that opens onto the unknown, part of

> the
> miracle
> of everyday

where the typography slows the forward momentum of syntax by putting space between words and making them strange. Thus form follows content; or, as Charles Olson put it, 'form is never more than an extension of content'. The forms of expression Torrance uses are various; they change according to the matter in hand, using different types of layout and language. At the end of the poem quoted above – the title is 'Bread & Wine' – the characteristic language and rhythm of the Blues can be heard, as the poet makes a decision to leave London:

> going to leave this town, anyway, &
> all this damn grass, pack up
> my books & poems in a box
>
> ragman, boneman, junkman
> can have my memories [...]
>
> going to leave this town
> cherry trees in blossom
>
> (GOPR 17)

And so he walks away from it.

The next phase is Bristol, the location of *Aries Under Saturn and Beyond* (1969), a book whose astrological title registers a drift in Torrance's work towards certain larger scenes of interpretation in the telling of life. Yet the big words are not allowed to take over from the detail of everyday living, which humorously cuts short any rising pretentiousness:

> Buddhas of Ages
> Buddhas of the Rocks
> daws swirling the
> trees in their own silent world
> of reaching
>
> the Buddha's hour, or
> reading the tea leaves, or
> spring surging from the treetops
> of a warm January gale
>
> (ASB 7)

The 'supergods/ themselves' are 'mortal giants', just as 'Buddhas starve/ in the cold wind': poetry, not religion, is the measure, the divination, of whatever comes. And that includes the interruption of joy by other things, as in this poem titled '(for Val', the name of his wife:

> she infects me with joy!
>
> I am a clumsy man
> who with what short sight
> steps upon taboos (or loves you) yeah,
>
> >   (and all the sophistry, & sociology
> >   hurts, makes his highs miserable)

(*ASB* 13)

This is not the well-worn idea of the poetic versus the un-poetic (who is the judge?), but an abandonment of filters and boundaries, such that the heady air of hot July is not siphoned off into a leak-proof container (called Poetry) but left unprotected:

> blanching mildew warm when stirred
> clumsy white moths july heat fecund
> heavy air sheets
> hang limp the kids
> are out from school the park
> patrolman wears a hard hat

(*ASB* 21)

The rhythm, regular at first ('blanching mildew ... '), laying things out in orderly fashion, is thrown out by an incursion of piled up words ('clumsy white moths july ... '), becomes syncopated as the beat gets delayed, like the opening phrases of a Charlie Parker solo, everything crowding in. The larger environment comes into intimate lyrical feeling, as it does in Lee Harwood's poems from this time: one of Torrance's poems is titled 'Poem (for Lee Harwood)', and playfully borrows Harwood's use of fictions.

Similar dilemmas occur, in 'Poem – Summer', with gardening – his job to 'keep back the wild growths// (but not/ in my head' (*ASB* 21) – a conflict between survival in the society and what inner life demands. He had written in the previous book: 'I have been busy with affairs/ of the sun winter, of the wretched work/ acquiring the further means to survive// of the spirit, acquiring its food/ from the sunwoods, busy with light' (*GOPR* 21). The ambiguities are strange: what work makes it possible for the spirit to survive, waged labour or being 'busy with light'? Spiritual work or physical? There is no resolution, only the flash, perhaps, of a possibility that the two might be the same, which would be the Golden Age or something like paradise, where work would be human self-creation. Meantime, poetry is that work: 'yes/ *this*/ is all real/ phenomena/ of the external world/ cycle/ of the seasons swirling [...]// the miracle/ of existence' (*ASB* 21–2).

Thus the lyric is not passive outpouring but work, decisions, even – or especially – where love is concerned, as in 'Love Poem' (also dedicated to Lee Harwood), where 'I come again/ to the perennial problem/ of just how to love you/ & again can only think/ that loving you is not grasping you/ at all/ which is in itself/ a form of knowledge of you' (*ASB* 36). The self and its actions are the material to be worked, not necessarily coherent or consistent ('"I am not/ confused."/ But I was'), not gathered into unity in the mirror of confession (Torrance was brought up a Catholic), which gets debunked ('I'm just a natural born/ SINNAH') (*ASB* 24). The writing is immensely intimate, by dint not of confession but of expenditure. Self is not outside the poem, something to be expressed, but occurs in time as the poem occurs. The poem, immersed in time, is an interrelation of decisions and chance, of intentions (to write a love poem) and random events:

> it's the formation of a
> coherent, choate love
> poem for you, my dear
>   pins of ice against the glass
>
> cars whoosh by in the street
> outside   the wind
>   blows again a   clock
>   strikes   a candle burns
>
>   (*ASB* 25)

The gaps in the typography register the uncertain relations between things, in contrast with the ideal of a 'choate love poem', where choate means fully developed and complete – Torrance's poem deliberately stands incomplete, with gaps, like Harwood's work.

Yet although Torrance treats the self as an occurrence in time, rather than as something that ought to be coherent, he does not abandon the idea of a progression or journey. The title 'Aries

Under Saturn' signals an astrological phase, to be succeeded at some point by another one, with a different meaning: so Torrance's title locates the poems inside larger movements. And in that connection there arises the question of whether to 'stay here in the city' or 'live wild with Basho out on the rocks?' (*ASB* 23) The debate is expressed with a degree of self-mockery ('I'm very happy/ helpless in the grip of a Western barbarism/ I can't quite replace with zen'), yet the point is serious. The Japanese poet Basho's isolation in wild nature was rewarded with the fine poems he was given to write.

We next find Torrance in an isolated farmhouse in mid Wales, in a book whose subtitle (*Poems, Glynmercher Isaf, June 1970 to October 1972*) locates it precisely in space and time. The book includes six photographs of the poet and the house, and begins with a round map, showing the house in the centre but nothing else except rivers and geological features marked by different shading. No roads, footpaths, or signs of human habitation, apart from the poet's house, are marked. This map shows the extent of the chosen solitude, its measure of erasure for the sake of acceding to a new plane. Here, moreover, he will need the earth for survival, work will be for self-sufficiency, equilibrium between the soil, the seasons, and the spirit.

The poems are arranged as a sequence marked by the calendar, and can be read as a progression that passes through phases of self, land, weather, and sky. The opening poem, 'The New Territory' has the subtitle '(In transit Bristol – Wales June 1970)'. The journey, like the book, is a sequence but also something else, less ordered. It begins with the convulsions of lovers' 'wrapt, hot bodies', 'thigh hooked over thigh', on 'the short turf', in 'clear, bland air', under 'skin-blistering sun': the lyric heat turned up another notch (*TH* 329). Thus the energies and the terrain. And in the midst of them the distances between seeing, inner vision, and matter collapse:

> the red & green phantoms leap across the fall
>
> a butterfly alights briefly on the meniscus
> to drink before flying off
>
> the magic glass swayed by a ripple
> – within the instant of its thought
> comes birthing at the surface, at the rib-point
> a life of no more deception, of no more lies!

The 'phantoms' are luminous emanations of superabundance, unwilled and insubordinate; in Christian parlance, 'grace', a gift received but not earned. That gift, in excess of any cause, will colour the whole book. It permits a dense interfusion of self and world such that the distance between thought and matter closes. Everything exists very close up: if 'meniscus' means a convex lens, then here it is the tiny place where a butterfly stands on water, upheld by the curved surface tension. The eye is very close to the thing seen, not engaged in measuring distances and angles between the body and the world, which is what set philosophy going. It could as well be one eye as two, or indeed many. And part of the gift is that the medium in which things stand forth, 'the magic glass' (where glass can be read as water, lens, and mirror), is also the medium of thought: the 'birthing' of matter and of thought have become one and the same event. This is the condition for 'no more lies', a statement having nothing to do with realism: realism depends upon representations held to be true, whereas here representation and the thing represented are on the same plane, are events of the same surface. The rhythm (three full beats: nó móre líes) is a signature that repeats through the book ('queen wasp flops', 'black fur throat', 'moon so slow'): the signature of surfeit.

The journey from Bristol accomplished, the cycle of poems begins in September, with figures of energy extended within the expanse of the sky and the long movement of the seasons:

> Into a clear blue sky
> hail granules stand like sculpture
> Floating amongst us half-hid
> the calyx, the unexploded shell
> of the flower   (TH 330)

– a suspension of forms in gravity and in air, the hail about to melt, the bud enclosed in a whorl of sepals about to explode, but more slowly, possessed of a long rhythm. The inner life is suspended between both rhythms, the immediate and the longer one: 'my heart too, dreamily/ suspires open'. The moment is in balance with the longer span: a slow explosion of energy. Two changes have happened in relation to the previous books: the earlier poems followed a development of one moment of inner life into another; they were organized along an evolving continuity of consciousness. Here the continuity is broken: the over-seeing eye has merged with the emergent world, and there is no one left to be the one who surveys:[3] 'judgement' has become 'its own madder yellow', as he will write in a subsequent poem (*TH* 333). Continuity requires a place it can be registered from: here there is no such place. This is where the second change comes in: the surface on which events are recorded is now the sensuous physicality of nature: the mind thrown against that, without the order and purposes of the city.

Against that backdrop, objects emerge with unusual sensual intensity, like the manifold varieties of mushroom which appear in autumn, some with a capacity to induce hallucination, such as

> pretty, intoxicant
> *amanita muscaria* emerging
> richly red from her
> silky membranous fur.
>
> (*TH* 332)

The poem begins with self-mockery which is generous rather than mean: 'Strode out into the woods with/ cat, axe & saw to bring back/ mushrooms.' What could 'cat, axe & saw' possibly have to do with collecting mushrooms which as everyone knows come up with a light pull of the fingers? An axe and a saw belong to the world of hard work, cutting and chopping firewood for survival; mushrooms offer themselves freely to the gathering hand, they belong to the world of luxury and not to the ordinary ('ordinary' relates to order and regularity). The difference runs through the poem, in varied shapes, as when 'preferring "my ease/ to my will" (Valéry)/ nettle & marigold beer/ trickles down my throat', where 'trickles' points to unstinting luxury, free from the anxiety which might cause one to gulp it down. Ultimately, the poet is luxuriating in time, wasting it. The slow abundance is fully inclusive of himself:

> My beard has grown
> as lushly as my garden. The fire
> hisses & flares. The fire in my head
> is a crippled demon I am burning up.

This, as well as hearth fire, can be taken as Heraclitean fire, the fire which for the ancient Greek philosopher Heraclitus was the basic substance of the universe: the universe in the hearth – and in the head. The universe is over-abundant, and excessive to any end in mind: to be human is to be its fuel, as well as capable of thought. You would think that the way to escape being mere fuel is to increase resources, accumulate means of production, and so assert human will over nature.[4] Yet the logic of Torrance's position is different: to listen unrestrictedly to the final sentence of the poem quoted above is to hear more than one meaning: 'I' is actively burning up the demon as fuel and yet 'I' *is* the demon, is the thing burning up. Thus 'I' is the conscious self but also the whole being, not fully knowable except by dint of burning up, in the very act of being consumed. Thus the self that is knowable by accumulation of knowledge is not the whole. The reality that is known in its burning up is not interpretable, cannot find an image ('the/ music becomes more insane, more unreadable').

Torrance's poem can be read as a response to Gerard Manley Hopkins's poem 'That Nature is a Heraclitean Fire and of the comfort of the Resurrection' (1888). For Hopkins, 'million-fuelèd, nature's bonfire burns on', yet 'her cleverest-selvèd spark/ Man, how fast his firedint, his mark on mind, is gone!'[5] And this brings grief, 'joyless days, dejection'. Only the Resurrection permits knowledge to transcend the destruction of flesh to 'ash'. Death also is in Torrance's poem, but without resurrection. Both poets, though, delight in the sensuous detail of sky and earth, as when Hopkins sees mushrooms in the clouds: 'Cloud-puffball, torn tufts, tossed pillows flaunt forth.' And both abandon an idea of accumulating time inside some sort of banking system that deals in lasting symbols. A key difference is to be found in the fact that there is a point at which, in Torrance's poems, interpretation breaks down and 'the/ music becomes [...] unreadable'. The interpretability of the world as signs ('dint', 'mark', 'shape' in Hopkins) fails in Torrance; the expenditure of living becomes without measure ('the insatiable fire'), while in Hopkins resurrection becomes the measure of life, the continuity that guarantees meaning: 'This Jack, joke, poor potsherd, patch, matchwood, immortal diamond,/ Is immortal diamond.' Hopkins's 'Is' is the *is* of resurrection.

A contiguous poem begins playfully with a quotation from a book about the usefulness of mushrooms as food: 'It is difficult to exaggerate the importance of mushrooms as food, for they contain ergosterol in large quantities – this is the raw material as it were of Vitamin D.' The staid and earnest prose, whose first phrase is borrowed for the title of the poem, embodies the stabilities of discourse, not the eye-to-eye meeting of mushroom and self:

> spore print of mushroom in the retina, in my dreams
> lens displacement in the multi-cellular dark
> abyssal sound of leaves in the wind
> rushing cloud dance before the sky closes in
>
> (*TH* 334)

Mushroom spores become direct trace on the retina, without the mind intervening, tactile more than visual. If nature is a backdrop, it also writes itself directly onto the body's most sensitive recording surface, the retina, which is of course a direct extension of the brain. Given, moreover, that spores are so tiny as to be virtually invisible, the eye here is extremely close up, as in dream space, where there is little or no sense of relative distance – it's in the conscious retelling of dreams that we put them into ordinary space. There is a hint, too, of insect eyes, as in the multi-cellular lenses of certain insects, inhabiting the dark; and thus a suggestion of a multiple emergence of things,[6] giving the sense of an abyss because without dimensions (or having n dimensions). In all this, something happens to the body as it loses its usual spatial orientation, abandoning its gravitational organization and its symbolic centring on the perspectival eye: a 'dilated movement' as Jeremy Prynne calls it (*TH* 295).

Food is fuel and fuel is the concern of the poem which bears the title of the book. Two types of movement figure in it: movement subordinated to survival needs, to the gathering of energy, 'the tyranny of fuel', 'up & down, round & round' (*TH* 333); and a free, unsubordinated movement: 'meanderings'. The first is controlled by the idea of cause and effect: 'The causal cone's base weight/ presses down on me.' The word 'cone' carries a footnote which relates it to W. B. Yeats's use of it as a symbol and specifically to the notion that 'the cone represents the universe, with God at its base & the potentialities of matter at its point'. The base is matter become hyper-rationalized, totally knowable: it is 'all in comprehension', the footnote says. The other, meandering movement of Torrance's poem is random, not fully comprehensible.

'Acrospirical' is explained by Barry MacSweeney in his response to the book, whose main title is *Acrospirical Meanderings in a Tongue of the Time*,[7] as follows:

> To acrospire means to throw out the first leaf sprout (1616); acrospire in 1674 is the first leaf that appears when the grain sprouts; and the adjective acrospirical relates to the young leaf shoot of the barley inside the grain when barley is being used for malt. Malt is the grainlike barley germinated and dried in a kiln. It flavours and colours beer. (*TH* 325)

And so the word combines visual emergence with budding and with intoxication; 'acrospirical meanderings' fuses meanings of drunken purposelessness and profuse growth. As in dreams, the condensation of meaning is the other side of the unformed, the unpredictable. And 'in a tongue of the time', with its regular rhythm, subordinates expression to regulated time, our time. The rhythm of 'acrospírical' is a reverse echo of 'tóngue of the', and comes back, in the title poem, as 'a tinkle of lightning/ on radio circuits' – that is, as random sounds which counter 'the causal cone's base weight'. Thus the two movements, the predictable and the formless, interpenetrate: inside the recognizable, the unknown. The next phrase ('As clouds red/ over a stormy sunset shift') has a distinctly nineteenth-century pattern to it, but is followed by 'Squirrel twists away round the trunk/ under which I find *Boletus luridus* & *Russula atro purpurea*', taking a reader back into sudden emergences and rich sumptuousness (*purpurea* meaning the colour purple and the costly fabric worn by a person of royal rank). And that is followed by 'Hare whips from cover in fierce spray as I cross the wet field', combining unforeseen movement and the association of hares with madness. *Luridus*, for its part, means yellowish, but also having an unnatural glare, ominous, gaudy. And so the colour of mushrooms, with their staid Latin names, is married to that point where matter cannot be known by rational knowledge: 'Judgement its own madder yellow. The insatiable fire.' Instead of a life subordinated to the aim of self-preservation ('the tyranny of fuel'), or indeed to any goal, the sheer onrush of nature, of time without measure. If 'judgement' has to do not with what you know but how you know it – how you know anything – and if that itself is 'fire', then perhaps this is a condition in which the outside and the Other, in their most radical and unedited sense, are allowed to enter poetry and transform it.

In that condition where music has become 'unreadable' and judgement a 'madder yellow', there is nothing in between the I and the non-human: it is impossible to slide anything between them, any degree or type of interpretation. It is a state whose openness entails exposure to paranoia, since the body has become a non-differentiated surface ('lens displacement in the multi-cellular dark') open to immediate invasion by forces outside.[8] These things that impinge on the body can seem, to consciousness, to have an intention behind them, possibly a malign one, as in the paranoia of feeling persecuted. However, the phenomenon of persecution is a manifestation in fantasy of a more primary state, in which the ordinary boundaries of the body are no longer the boundaries of being, and it becomes – to use Torrance's word – 'shapeless'.

'Poem to the Three Laughing Sages' (dated 30 November 1970) mixes the weather and the land with dream:

> Ripples in the trough, trough after trough
> another wave, another blow, another drench
> lichen and moss in an ever-wet land. The pineal drops
> where dreams slide
> whose hectic current washes & swamps me
>
> (TH 336)

The unceasing waves of weather make a rhythm which extends into dreams, though dream is both slower ('the pineal drops/ where dreams slide') and faster ('hectic current') in its several tempos, and thus more turbulent and unplottable. Pineal refers to the gland at the top of the skull, which in some vertebrates forms a light-sensitive third eye that responds to circadian rhythms. For Georges Bataille, in his essay 'The Pineal Eye', it permits the immediate entry of the sun into the body, 'a fire that eats the head', an 'expenditure'; it is highly erotic ('a giant [...] pink penis, drunk with the sun') and tears the body inside out: 'vision [...] is torn out and torn apart by the sunblasts into which it stares.'[9] Certainly, the body in Torrance's writing shares with Bataille's the erasure of boundaries. 'I would much rather try to be shapeless',[10] he writes in 'Quintessential Day', a desire which the poem counterposes to the 'iron-browed teachers of the law' which books ('lying in corners of the room') are described as. The poem declares its concern with 'the heavy, secret lies of the heart', which are placed immediately beside the final lines:

> Black raven wings brushing the sky,
> impacting air, fade slowly,
> beating in the blood.

(TH 335)

The relationship is metaphoric: that is, the 'heavy, secret lies' discover similarities in the dark wings against the light of the sky. But this is not metaphor in its usual current sense of decoration and value added, making things more 'meaningful', as in common parlance. If the wings are read as what sustains a body in a medium (air) which subsequently becomes blood inside a body, then internal and external surfaces have become confused with each other. It is similar to the way in which mushrooms imprint themselves 'in the retina', 'in [...] dreams', and 'in the multi-cellular dark', locating the eyes out there as much as inside the body. The metaphors become doors to pass through and nature itself a membrane.

The relation of lyric to everyday reality is one of the factors which has made lyric poetry problematic since around the mid twentieth century, though the difficulty began to take shape at the time of the First World War. Does not lyric present an ideal world, without factories, slums, ugliness, war; in other words without the real drudgery and undistinguishedness of mundane life? And does not that make it the province of the 'gentry', who do not suffer those things (which are the problem of the masses) or else are able from their distance to be ironical about them? It is a question both of politics and of ways of writing. Torrance's 'Day-by-Day Poem' takes up the issue of poetic method and begins by trying out various options:

> With the radium-tipped drill she
> No no it's not artificiality I want
> nor a flowing catalogue of nature
> Just look at these picture frames
> 'January & February when everything
> is in its chastest winter absence' writes John

(TH 337)

These initial lines are concerned with truth and language, in the sense of how truth can come about in language; neither futuristic artificiality nor backwards-looking pastoral will work. The lines taken from fellow poet John Hall gather attention towards seeing, and what frame seeing happens inside of. '"Why from this window am I watching leaves?"/ (Barbara Guest) "Am I to understand change, whether/ remarkable or hidden? ... "' The window embodies the selecting and gathering that transforms change away from randomness into understanding. It places that work of transformation in everyday life. But Torrance goes further and writes, 'the everyday mundane become lambent/ The cats have shat on the carpet again but I'm not depressed,/ thinking of the flowers of May'. 'Lambent' relates to a flame or light playing lightly upon a surface without burning it, and means softly radiant, licking. It turns seeing once again into touching, the surface of the actual, of occurrence, become radiant, succulent. As Barry MacSweeney wrote:

> the poems in this book shine with that 'original gift of spreading the atmosphere of the ideal world over familiar forms and incidents.' It is not the poetry of adorning the familiar with cute arabesques, but absolute fidelity to it. The poet's imagination communicates an air of marvel to the given. His communication with nature is a mutual one, 'the hiding places of infinite power.' A gathering which makes my real world spiritual, and my spiritual world real. So in this there is no feeling of the poems having been rushed, like battery hens, to meet some invisible demand [...] So in the reading we are not duped, by a quasi-religious glitter (say). (*TH* 325)

No more needs saying, except perhaps to recall Torrance's phrase, 'the everyday mundane become lambent', and read it as a reflection on poetry. Torrance's poetry does not transform the mundane by 'stopping time' in the sense of selecting the content of one moment and raising it up above ordinary time. That approach makes a profit out of the moment which can then be spread over the rest of life like some sort of glitter, just as capital makes out of human time the alluring but parasitic time of money and commodities. Torrance's way involves real risk: he exposes himself to the failure of vision, the sheer unilluminated plod of the day-to-day. A morality here, then.

'Spinning the Poem' continues these reflections, presenting the poet in the act of discerning patterns out of a scrambled sky ('concerned with the brew in the sky' (*TH* 349)) or identifying 'patriarchs & scribes & buglers' among the herd of cattle who 'look in the gate'. It is an act of selecting and ordering but counterbalanced by heady intoxication ('peppery scent of/ neon pink lupins/ foundering in raindrops'), tradition holding that lupins are narcotic, and by sheer animality: 'the bull sidles up behind/ his fancy & laps a mouthful of urine.' Discernment runs into disorder and the poem responds by distinguishing two types of relationship with time:

> He makes sounds
> in my head as I
> press a flower in a book with a midge
> a dried cadaver that falls out a year later

There is the bull's sound – animal, non-signifying – which belongs to the immediate moment, and there is also the midge preserved in a book, the latter a scenario in miniature of the potentiality of the book (i.e. poetry) to embalm objects. As Jack Spicer, a poet whom Torrance was reading at the time, wrote:

> We want to transfer the immediate object, the immediate emotion to the poem – and yet the immediate always has hundreds of its own words clinging to it, short-lived and tenacious as barnacles. And it is wrong to scrape them off and substitute others [...] The words around the immediate shrivel and decay like flesh around the body. No mummy-sheet of tradition can be used to stop the process. Objects, words must be led across time not preserved against it.[11]

Torrance presents the act of writing as taking place within a tension between two propositions: time preserved and time unmitigated, time made into ordered pattern and time spent in intoxication, in the pure meaningless noise of the animal. The tension is complicated by a hint of hermetic mysteries in which the body dies but the Word endures, and in a contrasting sense by the fact that the flower and the midge make an enduring material trace – and writing is an enduring material trace – so that one side of the opposition crosses over into the other, the embalmed 'cadaver' into the Word.

'Aries' (*TH* 338) has Torrance staring 'at rams in the fields/ & in the intervals sawing logs'; staring as if dazed or 'straight from sleep' (the title of another poem from the same months), without that comprehension which places things in an order of time management. The poem reverses the usual relation between work and leisure: the sawing is done 'in the intervals'. The poem moves between luxury ('the warbling of the hallucinatory chaffinch') and necessity, and ends with coming down from a 'high' which, given the use of the word 'acid' elsewhere in the book, might be related to LSD. Torrance's approach to drug experiences is to place them alongside everything else, neither elevating nor denigrating them. He is interested in the whole, all sides of reality. Thus the poem 'Straight from Sleep', mentioned above, begins with mess and chaos; they are the actual which counteracts the self's attempts to produce meaningful sequence:

> straight from sleep
> to chase sheep from the garden
> a bloody, dead blackbird on the doormat
> 'mid thousands of feathers & catspew
> the world jumps
> from this to that
> to break the ennui
> of my own tense control
> all goes into the melting pot of acid
>
> (*TH* 339)

The energy is excessive to ordered sequence, its meaning cannot be captured in that way: 'what to do with all this energy, lambent, unreconciled?' The poem presents us with two types of possibility, capture by regulated time and what exceeds regularity ('the planet helpless with mirth/ gold coins rolling in the streets'). And what is poetry, the first or the second: patterned sequence or what won't fit into pattern? More pointedly, which category does this poem belong to? The answer is both: it makes a patterned sequence of words and sounds, is recognizable as a type of lyric, but is also turned towards the outside, towards what cannot be contained in that form. And thus the Shelleyan ending ('the skylark's interminable raga/ borne aloft on shivering wings') may be read alongside the un-Romantic beginning, as an index of the distance traveled by English poetry since the early nineteenth century, with the unpoetic outside ('catspew', etc.) now included in the poem.

The poet's wife, Val Torrance, herself a poet, is included in the book not merely as a figure in some of the poems but as the maker of the round map and of the several illustrations, which unfortunately do no feature in *The Tempers of Hazard*. Moreover, as partner in the move from Bristol, she is a collaborator not just in the artwork but in the living, though, perhaps by the same token, she figures less as an actual subject in this book than in the previous one or in *The Diary of Palug's Cat*, which responds to the failure of the marriage. She belongs to the mundane, as author of necessary – but unheeded – advice, as when the author comes home drunk and starts to fill a pipe: '"If you take that you're/ going to be sick" said Val. "Yes,"/ I said, & lit the pipe. I was sick' ('Spirit of the May Days'; not in *TH*).[12] She is called 'The Candlemistress' (not in *TH*) which refers to her work making candles, but also 'the Moon-Woman' (*TH* 348), the erotic force within the planetary cycle, 'glittering Venus [...] the prize of man's imagination', mistress of mutabilities of weather, landscape, and the night sky.

Within the cycle of the sun, midsummer comes as a slow fullness, a suspension ('the temblor, the undammed current/ this waiting' (*TH* 341)), not anxious but overflowing:

> the moon so slow!   the deep summer moon!
> the bull gibbering & slavering on the slope at dawn
> rubbing his prick up against some tree stump in frustration

These midsummer poems are the high point of the erotic and lyrical arc ('The full tidal flow of summer/ rushes in the crowns of the trees' (*TH* 340)), the time of fullest luxury of the senses ('woodcock snuffling in the blue of half-dark'). Space is not given as an organization of distance in order to place things in perspective, but as dense, thick, roiling expanse: 'the air is soup, blue-dark, insect haze/ & we move through it, hands flapping', which produces a lovely dissolve of the body-image into the physical medium, redistributed into matter, matter which is, in Bataille's phrase, 'nonlogical difference'.[13] Midsummer is a time of maximum torpor and maximum incandescence, when the self is at its most dispersed: 'I am so many people I am not I am everybody else' (*TH* 341). And in this, the poet is seen humorously, as surplus to requirements, not contributing to any useful production: 'poets kick their feet around the place &

fertilize the queen/ the old poet drones, the old pranksters, lurking around with/ a sly fiddle & a little ditty air'. What is the queen? The principle of generation? The sheer surfeit of nature? The queen and the pranksters perform the two rhythms that traverse the book: the one slow, heavy, surfeited and the other light, rapid, playful.

October (1971) is mushroom season again, and 'Mushroom Fever' has 'the conflagration of opposites' coming out of 'the obstinate soil of myself' (*TH* 343). But although the conjunction of opposites is in alchemy the phase of greatest transformation, no such transformation occurs, but rather a failure of vision, a landing 'back in a prefabricated land': 'the problem is me', a line which is repeated three times. Yet the mood is not constant and out of the movement of birds and dreams, 'all tumbled together', in a 'slow-metalled dance', there surges up once again the superabundant event: 'fieldfares, spouting across the sky, surprised & delighted us' (*TH* 344).

Contrasts are laid down as a reader moves from poem to poem: the lyrical movement that extends across the separate poems makes them a kind of procession before the mind's eye that accompanies the changes of season: 'endless/ Robins, fierce, & twinkling, & paranoid' (*TH* 344); 'today's ditches crammed with spawn/ [...] brassy glare/ of the sun' (*TH* 345); 'the Ice Saints of May/ rear their anvilous heads/ about the horizon' (*TH* 347). The procession of the astrological year is also marked ('Now sol steadies/ to go back/ to those low, spectral emanations/ of December' (*TH* 348)), and counterpointed by the narrative of a life in its locality and its vagaries or 'meanderings', such as 'sitting out with a beer, it's too nice/ to stop drinking for the sake of/ a few intellectual scruples' (*TH* 348). Sometimes all the rhythms of time (everyday, seasonal, zodiacal) slow almost to a cessation of movement ('the moon so slow!' (*TH* 341)), the words pile up ('the brew in the sky/ the physic of that dimension, crucible'), and the senses overflow ('peppery scent of/ neon pink lupins foundering in raindrops' on top of 'sticky flies & a frog or two'), without narrative to provide rungs for the interpretative mind. *Acrospirical Meanderings* hits a reader at those habit-forming segmentings of the real, where language makes sense of life but takes away its stronger and more heady meanings. The poetry meets us at the narcotic gates or receptors, not so as to close down perception but to swim in the excess which narrative habits and the great biographical soap opera drain off.

The high intoxication of Torrance's poems carries a risk, that the self may be lost, and that its job of gathering and garnering experience, a biography, a CV, may become impossible. It's the condition of Coleridge's poet, mad in the eyes of others, drunk on his own vision: 'Weave a circle round him thrice,/ And close your eyes with holy dread,/ For he on honey-dew hath fed,/ And drunk the milk of Paradise.' One of the keys to Torrance's lyric exuberance is the sheer expenditure of energy without aim or goal, a form of power shunned by the anxious society of the fifties in England – and once again by the neo-liberal Thatcher epoch. Yet after the vision, what will take its place? 'After the ecstasy, many doubts, a vacuum;// "Find the centre/ & there is a tower/ & the only way out is up"' (*TH* 351). The old sky-centre symbol that comes to usurp the place of ecstasy, speaks of a danger. Torrance's poems are haunted by presences in the sky, as in the early 'Carshalton Poems': 'A strategist/ floats purposefully around in the/ blue sky' (*GOPR* 10). Yet his first book had begun by insisting 'That the affairs of man be planned/ by gods I do not, I do/ not/ accept', and then adding:

> unplanned,
>   unprofitable
>
>   untethered
>   unsaddled
>   unowned
> (alone & beside hysteria
>   but quiet
>
>   (*GOPR* 7)

The seven negatives insist there is no one to order, control, or appropriate, if you don't want there to be. They invite us in to the land of pure disorder, of wild pleasure, and yet the very insistence of saying no repeatedly exposes us to what is denied, to invasion by some controlling power or god: the stakes are raised.

What Torrance seeks to undo is a deep-seated inertia which he finds in himself, and which pits itself against the creative imagination. But its remedy is not 'keeping busy'. His poems enact a state of being almost dazed – 'straight from sleep' – yet combine it with a wide-eyed register of the environment: as Jeremy Prynne writes in the introductory note to the *Tempers of Hazard* selection of Torrance's work, 'The man walks in his sleep, yet he is there with almost abandoned precision' (*TH* 295). It is a fine line. Torrance's poetry, by its very exposure to nature, risks losing the other side of the poetic art: the transformation of materials. On the one hand there are the great, unalterable cycles of nature, pressing in upon the poet's habitation, his inertia, and on the other hand poetry as a transformative art, a type of magic or alchemy. Yet magic too carries with it the danger of the too rapid rush into pattern, into myth. The books that follow *Acrospirical Meanderings* trace out this dilemma, with a poetry that seeks to take responsibility for its relationship with its materials.

The Magic Door (Book 1) (1975) initiates the new phase: an ongoing cycle that to date consists of nine books.[14] The idea of a cycle implies a different way of reading from the one usually associated with lyric poetry. In its broad sense it demands that one does not extract from each individual poem a meaning to be enjoyed in separation from the other poems, but rather that one reads the poems as part of a larger action which may return to and modify its initial proposals, much as a life is shaped by foldings of time. It is an approach which American poets had insisted on more than British ones, though with important exceptions, such as David Jones's *In Parenthesis* (1937) and *The Anathemata* (1952) or Basil Bunting's *Briggflatts* (1965). Torrance's particular preoccupation with the relation between poem and book perhaps most closely resembles that of Spicer, whose work presses strongly against the limitations of the once-off lyric. Spicer writes against treating poems as 'one-night stands' and of his need for a different approach: 'It was not my anger or frustration that got in the way of my poetry but the fact that I viewed each anger and each frustration as unique – something to be converted into poetry as one would exchange foreign money.'[15] The moral is responsibility for the whole interchange of poetry and life over a period of time, instead of siphoning off sentiments into poems to be appreciated in isolation. 'Poems cannot live alone any more than we can,' writes Spicer. The conditions, material, social, and spiritual, that make the production of poetry possible are to be included in the work.

A cyclical or serial composition is not a linear sequence, where there is one line of causes and effects, but each event participates in various contexts, without giving exclusive centrality to any of them. The poems are placed in shifting relationship, without a single order. Thus Torrance's comments on his own composition call attention to the way the moment of everyday time exists inside other logics:

> always so confident we can retain
> the feel
>   of the moment
>
> & the year really did
> seem to turn in January, & we went remarkably fast
> into the light from the solstice
>
> (MD1 4)

The yearly cycle is of course familiar from the earlier books; what is different is the stated doubt about the self-sufficiency of the single moment and its correspondence with the larger orders. These, in *Acrospirical Meanderings*, came in the form of the movement of the seasons, the solar system, and astrological cycles making concentric circles around each moment of time. In the *Magic Door* cycle, the larger contexts include history, and can be discordant, sometimes humorously so.

Self-transformation is a major concern of the cycle. Book 1 explores correspondences between the stages of the alchemic process and those of inner experience; as Book 5 puts it, alchemists are 'seeking to transmute/ not gold but/ self' (*MD5* 11). The stages of transformation from everyday base matter to gold are symbolized in alchemy by colours; Jung, Torrance's main source, outlines the process:

> It begins with an unknown *materia prima* in the state of blackness (*nigredo*). Next in time comes the union [...] of contradictory principles, usually designated as [symbol for male] and [symbol for female]. There generally follows a disintegration or a death [...]; then the [...] whitening (*albedo*). [...] The next transformation is the reddening (*rubedo*). [...] the reddening is followed by the yellowing (*citrinitas*), the latter producing the coagulated, solid, or fluid gold.[16]

The idea of stages of transformation is indicated by Torrance's choice of titles for the five sections of Book 1: 'The House of

Stone', 'The Rubedo', 'The Transforming Substance', 'Terrain', 'The Nigredo'. These do not follow the alchemic sequence exactly: *nigredo* would come before *rubedo*, for example. Thus the book does not posit an orderly sequence; inherent in cyclical arrangement is the notion that life is not a single sequence but various, and that these may include the 'same' events but in a different order or that there may be 'a different view over the same scene at each full turn of the spiral', as Phil Maillard puts it.[17] 'The House of Stone', title and first line of section 1, gives a double meaning to stone: the material of the poet's house but also the alchemical stone, which, according to Jung's exposition, 'gives birth to itself', interweaving the possibilities of the self and of matter. In other words, the cycle begins with a phase of self and of matter in which figures of transformation begin to become available, as forms emerge out of chaos: 'chaos is a "confused mass" out of which the stone arises', as Jung puts it.[18]

These orientations can serve as a guide to reading the first page, which begins:

> The house of stone
> stuck
> like a worn & stubborn thumb
> in the Glen of Mercury
> buffeted by endless rainstorms

(*MD*1 3)

where 'Glynmercher', the name of the small valley in which the house stands, is translated into modern English, and Mercury (Roman equivalent of Hermes), the presiding spirit of alchemy, is named. The thumb makes the ambience lowly and not overserious – it could be a snook cocked at sky gods. The page continues with patternings of weather, trees, and lichen, forms emerging in their different scales, from the overarching sky to minute traces on tree bark ('etched fabric of cross-birch,/ cross-thorn & cross-alder/ mimicked by miniature frets/ of lichen outgrowths/ encrusted on/ dead birch twigs'), which suggest criss-crossing lines, picked out by the receptive eye – a way of reading nature. But not from an armchair:

> swinging amongst catkins in the fork of a hazel
> is the wind-stripped corpse of a dog fox
> hindquarters bared by weeks of galewash

> the naked balls hanging pathetic between
> thighs holed by death-blow or carrion creature

The body is swung between life and death, pattern and chaos, as the naked animal flesh draws a reader in to kinship with its intimacy.

The pattern can be momentary, like the 'fixed powder spicules/ draping out of white air' (*MD1* 4) which give a marvellously alive sense of gazing at snow and finding a delicate weave of particles held in the blinking of an eye. This is one of a series of crossovers between the instant of reading nature and that of writing. The texture of the book as a whole is made up of many different kinds of moment, including – in a part headed 'Letter to Lee' – those of daily work, such as 'Val digging her onion bed' and Torrance fetching manure (*MD1* 8), and so the meaning of the word 'everyday' becomes more inclusive than in *Acropsirical Meanderings*. The text is interleaved with several visual designs by Val Torrance, one of which combines the third hexagram from the *I Ching* with various ovular shapes.[19] The hexagram, which like all of them derives meaning from the chance throw of coins (originally yarrow sticks), is called 'Difficulty at the Beginning': 'the situation points to teeming, chaotic profusion [...] in the chaos [...] order is already implicit [...] the superior man has to arrange and organize the inchoate profusion of such times of beginning.'[20] This, then, indicates what is at stake in the poet's decisions that make the composition of the poem.

There are a number of self-reflective passages, more focussed and more sustained than any in the previous books, like this one:

> the trapped feeling remains. Not trapped here, geographically, but here, within myself. A feeling that waxes & wanes from one minute to the next. At the other extreme lies, I know, a joyous, carefree happiness, associated with loving Val, being involved with friends, poetry, dope; living this dream (*MD1* 17).

As Iain Sinclair, Torrance's publisher, observed, he is no longer 'so much *aroused* by the damp moorland. It is a condition of marriage; deeper in doubt, deeper in need.'[21] Growth is more than simply emergence, it requires a more sustained purpose, more study, more information; 'he is offering himself [,] to become a different *kind* of poet,' Sinclair notes, 'because so far everything has been generous, immediate, possessing not possessed. Now the effort will be of a new order; possessed, as Olson was, by an *urgency* of knowledge.'[22] In this sense, the cycle as a whole is informed by various types of knowledge, of which alchemical symbolism is only one. The others include mythology, history, geology, ecology.

Thus the scenario is of writing inside various interpretations of location, which include a distinction between the ego, 'desirous of fame' (*MD1* 15), and the more inclusive self with 'a somewhat core of dark/ patterns from the outside'. The book concludes with several dreams, 'still urban', as Sinclair slyly notes, of journeys to the metropolis ('suburban villas') and anxiety in different guises, such as running for a train: 'how many dreams/ of escaping trains were you involved in/ before you caught this one?' (*MD1* 45) Here the cycle spirals not towards transformation but into repetition: 'you go muttering round/ "There is no way out" or/ "There is no exit" but all the time/ the trap is you.' The longer project has to be capable of sustaining failure, not just the failure of its protagonist but of itself, but without ceasing to regenerate its own possibility out of the necessity of change.

Thus each book of the series finds new materials. Book 2 is called *Citrinas*, a word that indicates the final alchemical substance, gold. But the transformation is incomplete, and the writing, 'Seeking the/ bright mandala/ of the sun/ gold coin glimmering away/ above the roof of clouds' (*MD2* 6), finds itself at a threshold, where 'ghosts flicker/ at the very edges' (*MD2* 5). These ghosts, like Spicer's, are 'not the same as the dead', but 'a ghostly other', whence comes 'the real poetry [that] is beyond us [...] where the real edge of it is'.[23] Not 'on edge', which denotes anxiety, but the most delicate and detailed sense of strangeness, as with 'the/ odd spray of leaves suddenly yellowed or ghostly/ creamy-white like a moth's wing' (*MD2* 6). The protagonist also is found at an edge, 'teetering on the brink of dogma/ he turned back at the last moment', which describes an overall tension of this book: between the will to transformation and the trap of closed systems.

The main subject of that desire for secure belief are the pre-Roman standing stones and other 'antiquities' discovered in the vicinity, but first let us take in the various contentions between certainty and uncertainty. One section carries the heading 'Subsidence Was Pulsatory, However' (MD2 8), where 'pulsatory' refers to how even geological processes are not smooth or predictable. The composition here places discontinuous processes side by side: the rotting of leaves and apples; the erosion of the soil; 'bread rising on the hearth'; the logs burning up; the road that climbs out of the Glen of Mercury; the movement of birds; roadworks exposing the subsoil; the turbulent geological formation of the valley; and the 'progress of a large/ staggery black beetle across the floor' – this last once again counterposing the smooth with the lumpy. The contrast is reflected in the diction: on the one hand the latinate vocabulary (such as 'subsidence', 'pulsatory', 'eroding', 'progress') offering the purchase of concept over matter, and on the other the Anglo-Saxon ('wink', 'rot', 'stench', 'staggery', 'turfy') registering that which eludes or exceeds concept. The first sorts and classifies (as the *nigredo* and *rubedo* of alchemy do, for example) and the second offers non-classifying words like '*lumpy* cloud', '*scrambly* terrain' (MD2 13, 27). The Roman inheritance gives progress, and the other the cared-for and non-prestigious details of material existence.

Geology moves into alchemy and inner life: incomplete, and unpredictable; 'these quirks &/ despairing heaves/ of the unstable compound/ & each time gulfs open/ that you never knew were there' (MD2 10) – neither smooth nor guaranteed. The standing stones on the other hand seem to answer a desire for spiritual certainty. They offer themselves as condensations of the sacred, traversing the terrain with tracks of paranormal energy that antiquarians have called ley-lines. They are first mentioned by Torrance in a narrative passage about searching for a particular standing stone in the Brecons and finding a 'labyrinthine housing estate [...] swallowing up that ley', though he eventually stumbles across that 'hoary monolith', 'well guarded by brambles' (MD2 18, 19). There is self-mocking humour in the details ('hoary' being a cliché for venerable) but it does not take away the keenness of the pursuit. There is a photograph of a standing stone on the cover of the book, and another on the frontispiece. The third photograph, interleaved in the text, is a close-up of a vertical piece of wood, stripped of its bark, scored with the meandering tracks of small insects or worms. The visual invitation prepares one for the textual one: to find in the meandering grooves by which parasites interfere with the vertical, the scrambled lines of housing estate labyrinth or of brambles. The obvious sense, of the sacred emptied by the modern, the 'hoary monolith neatly desecrated by the recent inscription "BM"', is complicated by another one: the lure of religion dulled by the unpredictable complexity of the now.

A section headed 'Letter to Barry MacSweeney' (were the initials on the monolith his?) combines humorous references to Arthurian myth with detailed technical accounts of the geology of the zone. The theme is the discovery of what looks like a pre-Roman stone arch, which is shown in two photographs. It seems to be a reward for 'having always dreamed that I might find an "unknown" antiquity in this area' (*MD2* 27). But it turns out probably to have been built by the quarry manager who owned the house beside it, an example of '19th century Romantic cults' which went in for 'druidic architecture'. Rewarded with his antiquity, the poet is assailed by 'Immense/ doubt// In a sense/ Glan Yr Afon is/ corny// as though I had been/ fooled/ by it ... ' (*MD2* 30) The discovery of the stone arch and subsequently of its Romantic provenance is told with some *frisson*: there is an edginess to the narrative which holds the humour in check. But the final section of the book, called 'Mirages', puts humour uppermost. It tells of a return trip to London, the poet 'Distrustful of this Celtic/Arthurian/ley-line/gothic obsession' (*MD2* 36), as the train slides into Paddington. Instead of a sacred order, there are only 'the scraps of old leys, their power gone, or vanquished, back alleys stinking of dog pee. Everything *crawls*. & its dust & confusion & manic screams & entrails all over the place.'

Book 3 of *The Magic Door*, with the title *The Diary of Palug's Cat* (1980), has as its main narrative events the breakdown of marriage and a later brief affair, interwoven with dreams of ancient places of power and with ongoing geological investigations. The absent wife belongs to the ideal world: 'divination/ from the flight of sparks/ up the chimney/ I dance/ with the image of Her ... ' (*MD3* 5). The writer, meanwhile, is 'drowning in/ flu slurry' (*MD3* 7), the semi-comic title of Part I being 'Flu Concerto (for the band)', the last presumably a reference to the fact that Torrance had begun to perform and record with a rock band. There is a certain wordiness sometimes, perhaps coming out of the need to recuperate capabilities, beginning with talk, but there are also some lovely humorous passages, as when the landlord, Rhys, comes to visit and his conversation is noted:

> It's good that people drink, it helps the kidneys. It's good that people smoke tobacco, it keeps thousands of negroes employed. We discuss the economy & agree that nothing has changed since the forties. Well, it'll all end soon, he says, there isn't much more time (*MD3* 26)

But as the book ends, Torrance's ability for lyric condensation, no longer covered by talk, becomes sovereign:

> the blonde grasses
> flicking imperiously
>
> the brilliance
> rising from the ground
>
> the horizon
> dissolving in my backbone
>
> (*MD3* 55)

The most historical part of the cycle involves the semi-mythical dynasty of Brychan, a Welsh epic hero, and draws on early Welsh sources such as *The Triads* and Geoffrey of Monmouth.[24] Given the degree of uncertainty about the data, 'it's a great field for the imagination'. Torrance follows this comment with a description of his method for composing *The Book of Brychan* (1982), which is Book 4 of *The Magic Door*:

> You take the basic carpet weave and reweave it, according to your current-model consciousness of history. Having delved so much into all that Dark Ages stuff, it's as if I can see it as a totally illuminated script that I can unpeel in front of my eyes at any time; which of course I can then weave backwards and forwards into European history, into Mediterranean history, into pre-history.[25]

The idea of weaving and reweaving is given visual shape in the first illuminated letter of the book: it takes the form of a Celtic interlace, made out of the body and head of a snake. After a slow introit of one-word lines the writing negotiates a shift to words with a certain mythological glow, like litany, wisdom, pyramid, altar stone, temples. There is, however, a harder edge, as layers of history and of inner life surface simultaneously:

>   mashing, planing, & smoothing
>   the onion bed
>   a pig's tusk, shards
>   of a coarse red pottery surfacing
>   I am at the
>   blind point of history discharging
>
>   Lunar   tides
>
>   move in our   blood
>
>   (*MD*4 15–17)

It is the past emerging as energy in the everyday now: it breaks into and alters the present. Yet this sense of history as contingent material traces is placed alongside cosmic constants ('lunar tides'), which bring in a stratum of invariability and certainty. And yet the book does not attempt to overrule the layeredness of historical narratives, and this removes any possibility of single, stable meaning. Thus early Christianity is taken to be 'a patina/ warped & woofed upon/ the more ancient palimpsest of druidism' (*MD*4 27). And the precariousness of meaning and the belief in the permanence of poetry ride uncertainly alongside each other as 'I consult the leaning maen/ at the crossroads, holed/ top & bottom   perhaps/ a very old railway sleeper/ definitely/ a sleeper// the capsule upended in the earth// the eternal poem in motion through time' (*MD*4 41). 'Capsule' suggests an esoteric dimension or covert invasion by aliens ('sleeper'). And so *The Book of Brychan* yields a kind of double vision, where the collision between the ideal world and the actual modern environment produces crazed misrecognition.

Books 5 and 6, *The Slim Book / Wet Pulp* (1986), return to short lines and spare lyrical condensation. Words and things are more alone, as if freed from a larger mass. It is that 'birthing' which haunts all of Torrance's writing from *Acrospirical Meanderings* onwards, as the actuality of truth ('birthing at the surface, at the rib-point/ a life of no more deception, of no more lies!'). Now in *The Slim Book* the Word itself is born at the surface of writing but is also inherently unstable: 'the nature of the word/ the nature of logos// changing every second// [...] molecular frenzy' (*MD*5 15). Thus, in a geological metaphor, time is that which flashes up on the surface of the poem: 'time is a magma/ erupting/ to the surface of the lyric'. The reflections on poetics include a return to principles learned from Creeley and Pound, to handle words as 'shapes, glyphs [...] ideograms' (*MD5* 14), yielding chiselled blocks of sound and image, a lesson carried into British poetry by Basil Bunting through his apprenticeship to Pound. That concern with paring down to the essential, the necessary, carries over into *Wet Pulp*, which is made up of short, haiku-like pieces. They have three imaginary authors, who mingle characteristics of Torrance's writing with those of friends, and answer each other's poems, a figure of the pleasure in artistic collaboration which is the counterpart to his chosen isolation. The final section, the envoi, is authored by all three. This interweaving of persons, of voices, of languages has been characteristic of the whole cycle and here pays homage to the gathering of poets, friends, and visitors as well as acknowledging the community visited in books, without which it would not have been possible.

The chiselled nature of Book 5 applies as much to the emotional content as it does to the verbal form:

> the low sun
> reveals every grassblade
>
> soft patchword of fields
>   hill by hill
> leading to the mountains
>
> heartburst of tenderness at this
>
> 50,000 nuclear triggers
>   poised
> to rub it all to waste
>
>   (*MD5* 16)

What comes to the surface is the sharpest edge of an ongoing ecological concern with 'the damaged sphere' (*MD4* 49), 'the earthbound', the 'stink of fuel oil from the ocean', with which 'poets [...] must [...] stay in touch', the precarious material support that makes the spiritual possible. The ensemble of the cycle is more than its parts, as is the continuing work of the poet, which has needed more than half a lifetime.

3

Barry MacSweeney: The Fire-Crowned Terrain

> Poetry is cast as Song, as Dance, as Prayer, Lament, Curse, Rant, as instrument of desire: as instrument of rebellion
>
> (Maggie O'Sullivan)

Barry MacSweeney grew up in Newcastle where he had been born in 1948, and left school at 16 to become a newspaper reporter. He worked for tabloid papers, in the south as well as the north, for the rest of his life. He felt a very strong allegiance to the north-east, its language and history, yet at the same time his work draws on a wide range of enthusiasms, including Rimbaud, Shelley, Milton, Bunting, Russian revolutionary art, Apollinaire, Johnny Cash, the Doors, the heretics of the English Revolution. As Maggie O'Sullivan wrote, his work resounds 'with the spit of dissent and the edgy, wounded anger of revolt'.[1] It is written against the social amnesia, the 'spin', and institutionalized lying that have taken place in the name of modernization: especially against the language that anaesthetizes and makes submission easier. Against the identities that have been invented in order to facilitate consumer capitalism, he counters with allegiance to outsiders and the inadmissible. His first book, *The Boy from the Green Cabaret Tells of His Mother*, was published to considerable acclaim by a mainstream publisher (Hutchinson) in 1968, and he was even nominated, aged 20, to the Oxford Professorship of Poetry. He was abandoned by the literary establishment when he didn't go on writing what they wanted (something like a Geordie answer to the 'Liverpool poets': consumable, 'regional'). As Nicholas Johnson wrote, 'Barry MacSweeney was a contrary, lone wolf. For 25 years his work was marginalised and was absent from official records of poetry.'[2] He died in 2000.

His poem 'Brother Wolf' is an allegory of the poet as a 'rosy myth' to be consumed. By virtue of this myth, the early death of the artist figures as a price to be paid for nonconformity, making him an alluring figure to identify with, an ideal self that, far from interfering with the gaze of power, feeds it, with the payment it demands: a fantasy that allows us to go on living as before, because it covers over the real cost of adjustment. MacSweeney rejects this low-cost romanticism. If the early deaths of Chatterton, Shelley, Jim Morrison, Brian Jones, and others, were simply the price to be paid to society for rebelling, it would allow us to continue in resentful conformity. Instead, it is the cost of persisting in their desire. The reward is to know death, the death we live. Thus the inordinate speed and intensity of their lives, 'sixty miles an hour, backwards', like Chatterton, who 'leapt into the fire' (*WT* 23).

'The Last Bud', written when MacSweeney was 18, renounces the poetry of 'melancholic distance', the 'support' of 'verbal chicanery', the profit of 'sentiment', or 'piety' (*WT* 15–16). Instead, it asks, 'What happens when the legacy you search/ for, that supposed grail, wretches in your/ belly, leaving you weak-kneed and crying/ into a lavatory pan?' MacSweeney used to vomit before reading his poetry in public. Later, in *The Book of Demons*, it is alcohol that makes him vomit. But both are measure of his tremendous thirst for the real: 'the new reality, the real [...]/ kicks you over [...] leaves you for someone/ else but leaves no sentiment (spelled/ sediment), nothing to scrawl on sheets/ about'. Newcastle speech is the way he gets to the pun: sentiment as sediment. Poetry requires him to abjure 'things ... / false on the page, prostituted, wedged/ onto pedestals.' Instead of 'poets putting one/ another on stands, laughing a little,/ slap a back or two[,] Break a back or two/ then write about that'. He abjures the whole economy of poetry as a surplus to be skimmed off life, savoured, remembered. Instead, 'Down into the pit', entering the domain of death, for a different kind of knowledge: to see how the twisted bodies of the dead testify to the 'black cunning' which has worked on 'the soft heart', 'the plastic spine', turning the arrows of desire away from 'the aim'. Why does death make these things visible?

Because of its inverse illumination, its 'brilliant darkness'. The poet abjures 'your kingdom of light,' because he will not abandon his desire, whatever the cost.

MacSweeney's poems make high demands upon a reader. They do not offer an exchange of points of view, but the real expense of living. The movement towards that challenge starts to take shape in *Brother Wolf*, his 1972 book whose title invokes affinity with the animal whose intensities are a disturbance to the symbolic controls of language. 'Brother Wolf' is also a homage to Thomas Chatterton, the eighteenth-century British poet who broke with the southern latinized English inherited from Chaucer and made of northern English a vehicle for poetry. In 'Elegy for January', a talk on Chatterton given in 1970, MacSweeney said: 'You are the elegant, eloquent, poet, my brother! The creator of the most beautiful poetry. You are the wolf. I read again, and again: *Alas! I cannot sing – I howl – I cry!* What is there, after youth, but sleep, and death, and loss of instinctive beauty?'[3]

Brother Wolf tells how Chatterton, the young poet, is taken up and used by the literary establishment, on a basis of cost calculation:

> The whole of Chatterton's life presents a fund of useful instruction to young persons of brilliant and lively talents, and affords a strong dissuasive against that impetuosity of expectation, and those delusive hopes of success, founded upon the consciousness of genius and merit, which lead them to neglect the ordinary means of acquiring competence and independence.
>
> (WT 30)[4]

'Fund', 'affords', and 'means' translate Chatterton's life into the language of money and investment: useful items of exchange (instruction to young persons). 'Success' is the social prestige which has to be paid for in agreed ways, it has to be earned, the debt paid to those who have earned their power: these rules apply to poetry. Chatterton broke them and was made to pay the price.

MacSweeney turns these values upside down; first comes the lyric fire – energy – surging upwards:

> A young poet's life burns
> Presses
>   (july wind on Hartfell)
> taking our hearts (and poetry) higher
> as if to be cleaned
>
> (*WT* 24)

That is what comes first. The meaning, and who it belongs to, comes after, in a series of metaphors about being eaten. Chatterton's body is eaten by fish, like Shelley's heart, 'which later turned out to be/ Liver/ & the fish had a whale of a time munching english poetry/ It still happens'. The black humour produces openness to shock:

> taking our hearts (and poetry) higher
> as if to be cleaned
> & not one fish with an answer.   You can't expect advice
> from someone you eat then criticize for having bones
> because he wants to keep his body in shape & and not spread it
>   around
> all over the estuary
> (and poetry)
> Why Chatterton lived in the hills
>
> (*WT* 24–5)

The habit of ordinary reading would press one to take the metaphor as a resolution: Chatterton eaten by fish as a final horizon of meaning, the poet sacrificed to Nature – end of story. But the metaphor sticks in the gullet: Chatterton's body has bones to hold it together, it's real, it's not a thing to be consumed in order to produce meaning. What can't be swallowed (by the myth of the poet as sacrificial hero) is the material body, held together by bones in a medium that would otherwise destroy it. The poem switches not from one level of meaning to another, but from meaning to non-meaning, from meaning to sheer material (a body): the world upside down. It does this with a gesture of strange convulsive blankness ('because he wants to keep his body in shape and not spread it around'). A gesture is a communicative action, in this case a communication about communication itself, which declares, I will not enter into your language. The poem throws a spanner in the works of the well-oiled reading machine which extracts cost-free meaning out of poetry. The notion of body as food, because it echoes so strongly with the symbolism of sacrifice in the Christian Mass and earlier Orphic rituals, could easily swallow up the poem's meaning into myth. But the turn back to the material of the myth, to the actual unassimilable body, sticks in the gullet, impedes speech.

The impediment takes many forms, one of them being 'the randomness' of Chatterton's death, evident once the mythology crashes:

> [...] The randomness of (his) death
> the particular randomness
> of.   Towards which blood he ran the soft floor of his eye
> [...]
> Walpole slew. No rose. No honey
> suckle on the vine. The rain
> Hurt
> with its own
> soft density
> falls.
> No.
>
> (WT 28)

Eyeballing death, the poem comes into an extraordinary stillness of suspended shock. The empty space that follows 'the particular randomness/ of.' is not a Harwood-type suspension of meaning (the slow forming of a surface), but speaks of the force of an infinite event. The song ('Honeysuckle Rose') is broken, a denser music enters, and enters the place of pain. Unpacked into complete grammatical statements, the language would not penetrate to that area of sheer psychic vulnerability where the eye is close up to death and there is no lyric honey to be extracted – in what is a recurrent metaphor of the poem – by bees, those obedient and industrious creatures. The real expense is 'Hurt', which with a capital letter looks like the beginning of a sentence (and therefore a noun) but sounds like an adjective or verb. Is the rain itself hurt, as in a mythic version of nature? But it's the words themselves that fall, with 'soft density'; against the romantic myth of nature, words themselves become nature, i.e. 'the randomness of [...] death'.

MacSweeney's writing shares with Torrance's the wide-eyed, unfocused gaze. He even quotes Torrance's word, 'meniscus', though in Torrance that is where truth emerges ('a life of no more deception, of no more lies!'), and in MacSweeney it is the place where the fish heads feed on Chatterton's body ('The mullet used his body for a staircase// They float enviously around the meniscus on a raft of weeds'). The poem appears to speak of the ideal wrecked on the real:

> High hearts
> are wrecked.
> They fall on the rocks and the rocks
> fall on them.
> Wrecked.
> What are you doing?
> Telling you lies.
>
> (WT 28–9)

Clive Bush's gloss on this passage is that MacSweeney conceives Chatterton's death 'within a visionary framework whose *promise* is that the earth and the body are one', but that 'it is not so easy' for him, among other reasons because vision fails in the face of stony reason and 'the silent indifference of the world'.[5] But it is not a poem that tells of sustaining an ideal against a hostile world. That is not the narrative. The rocks *are* nature, they are not allegorical. Or, strictly speaking, they pass from being allegorical to falling through the net of interpretation. A gap is opened, not just in allegory but in language as such.

That Chatterton's 'eyes were stuck to mountains' (WT 23) opposes John Locke's eighteenth-century philosophy in which the senses are separated from things by 'secondary qualities'. These secondary qualities are analytic entities like hotness, coldness, colour, shape, size, and so on, which the mind grasps (as nouns) in order to know the world. As Basil Bunting argued in his 1930 essay on the English language, the splitting-off of qualities into separate entities is encouraged by the language, with its tendency to withdraw from the dense interrelatedness of things a sort of floating collection of aspects, abstract nouns to be manipulated at will, ideally by a manager, an ideas man. Bunting's remedy as a poet was twofold: syntactical complexity, learned from the Elizabethans and Latin poetry, in order to embody interrelatedness, and northern speech for its greater concreteness.[6] MacSweeney's answer is similar, though instead of using complicated syntax he opts for paratactical word clusters; that is, compacted groupings of words which do not obey formal grammar but whose interrelations are highly compressed and complicated.

Yet MacSweeney's writing does something that cannot be found in Bunting. Though a considerably older poet, born in 1900, Bunting was important for the British Poetry Revival because he had kept Modernism alive, against the anti-Modernist mainstream, carrying forward the lessons he had learned from Pound, bringing them into an English tradition and making them available to younger poets. But when MacSweeney wrote

> Chatterton's eyes were stuck to mountains.
> He saw fires where other men saw firewood.
> One step ahead in recognizing signals.
> And leapt into the fire.
>
> (WT 23)

he was entering new territory. This is not just a reversal of Locke, in that it takes the sense organs to be physically connected to matter, there is also a confusion between things and meaning:

> Chatterton (who was no lemming)
> mistook the hill
> for a green light.   Go! His final breakfast of pebbles.
> The mullet used his body for a staircase.

Chatterton, allegorical figure of the poet, crashes into the real. The membrane of language is torn: things have become meanings in themselves. It is a mistake, a delirium, but also an experience of truth. To call it madness would be to use the label of illness in order to disqualify. The Romantic poets' pantheism had been a way of restoring the infinite richness of the relation between nature and human mind against the reduction of nature by industrialism to material for production and consumption. Bunting's idea of nature as the 'histology of God' threw his belief in the minutely observed detail of the material world as the cell-structure of God, against the twentieth-century world of total administration. MacSweeney rereads and transforms that tradition inside and against late twentieth-century consumer society, the society where human beings happily consume their own participation. If things become meanings in themselves the whole order of symbolic capital, which makes culture into 'value added' to then be consumed, falls. This can happen only through a type of abrupt violence, like a flash of pain or joy which ordinary consciousness habitually shies away from. Only black humour, and the condensations that sheer away from normal statements into other speeds, towards the speed of death, hold together the ordinary and the tearing of the veil. A 'breakfast of pebbles' is the unassimilable inside the poem – not just unassimilable but the substance of an ecstatic materialism: to mistake 'the hill/ for a green light' recalls the emerald light of Rimbaud's *Illuminations*.⁷

Like an animal, a wolf, in timeless immediacy, MacSweeney's figure of the poet does not carve the environment into categories and thus save himself some costly errors. Everything has meaning, in a much more unselected way than in an environment filtered by language, by *this* language, the one of the society that attempts to consume him. The language of Locke, and its prolongations in Orwell's Newspeak and Thatcherblair Media speak, is the real delirium. Poetry is what 'the brain [...] needs to have/ to see' (*WT* 13). Hence – the unspoken question – what else could Chatterton do?

That the poet 'mistook the hill/ for a green light' needs to be placed with

> Chatterton knew
> you may not return to the source
> when you're
> it and
> died.
> At Sparty Lea the trees don't want Orpheus
> to invoke any magic
> they dance by themselves.
>
> (*WT* 25)

Sparty Lea, in the hills above Newcastle, was a 'sacred' place for MacSweeney. The phrases echo: 'dance by themselves', 'breakfast of pebbles'. There is no myth, or ideal, or even idea. Ideals and ideas belong to the people who thought Chatterton 'a rare catch': 'It's an Ideal which is an idea/ like eating your best friend' (*WT* 32). This is writing without sentiment/sediment.

MacSweeney himself insisted there was a clear distinction between the type of language he had used for *Brother Wolf* and the way he composed the *Odes*, which with regard to form is his most inventive book: 'I was aware that I really could not go back in using the kind of forms I was using in *Brother Wolf*, that sort of more strung-out form', which he also calls 'linear form'.[8] The changes are in fact various. One of the most important has to do with the shape of the poems on the page: most of them consist of short lines arranged around a vertical axis, rather than justified to the left margin. The shapes are spare, and sharp, the product of extreme condensation, beyond even Basil Bunting's recommendation to poets to 'cut out every word you dare' and 'do it again a week later, and again'. Take 'Beak Ode':

>   Open your black-backed gull.
>   See her, inside.
>
>   Fine bird,
>   hen.
>
>   Pearl
>   orange barley.
>
>   Shrink, wear partial vests
>   of stitchwort
>   campion
>   & lace.
>
>   (Filters red
>
>   &
>
>   blue.)
>
>   Cave
>   rime.
>
>   Mottled death,
>   &
>   Pan.
>
>   (WT 55)

The extreme condensation hones a seething dance of meaning to a fine edge. 'Rime', for example, has many possible senses and the poem does not urge a reader to choose one of them but rather to find what holds their centrifugal variousness together: frost or fog, rhythm, correspondence of sound and meaning. And the 'filters red// &// blue' might be sense organs, colours for theatre lights, coloured lenses, papers used in chemistry to test for acid, a love potion (philtre); or filters could be a verb (as might 'rime'), bringing about the effects associated with some or all of the meanings of the nouns. The other words ('open', 'see', 'shrink', and 'wear') are imperatives, and could be taken as instructions in alchemy or the preparation of a love philtre or other spell. The poem burgeons, rather than settling into any particular track. And the way the words are placed on the page is a 'cutting across meaning, not having words next to each other which are supposed to be there'.[9]

The high charge that runs through the words is what holds them together. It makes the body of the poem into a lightning rod that draws displacements of undifferentiated desire. Animal and vegetable realms inhabit the human senses, without separation, instead of nature dominated and filtered. This produces a plane where primary forms ('red// &// blue') operate, and where variation itself, lived, is openness to time ('Mottled death'), where wild nature and the human are joined ('Pan'). The poem's movement, its register of the displacements that pass through its language, is wholly incompatible with the speeded-up time of postmodern society, marked by rapid and uninterrupted succession of images and signals.[10] The pace of the *Odes* is, by contrast, immensely slowed down. The sheer amount of matter that the words gather in short space slows time. The final three lines of 'Beak Ode' take us to a mythic time, a thick time where change, known as history, ceases. And yet, the words make forms that matter rushes through ('Filters red/ &/ blue'): within the slowed-down time, there is high speed. But it is the speed and pitch of psychic life, as it breaks away from the accelerated punctuation of the everyday and receives the onrush of the cosmos. This is lived time, as opposed to time packaged for consumption.[11]

To fully unravel the semantic compression of a poem like 'Beak Ode' would take a lot of space, and that is the point: large stretches of the language have been cut away to leave shapes that pulse with strange force. Nature unselected, wrenched free from the mental map of the ordered selection of species, requires a self freed from the requirements of identity. In the poem under discussion, the eye or 'I' moves inside the bird's body as if it were a diorama, with swift change of scale ('shrink'), and entry into the sheer making of colour by the senses, and of sound (inner resonance of a body), and a breath-catching final condensation of varicoloured beauty, death, and the wild goat-god of ecstatic music. There was nothing like it in modern British poetry until Maggie O'Sullivan's work of the 1990s.

MacSweeney was highly aware of the difficulty, for himself as a writer, of what he was doing:

> I can write a narrative poem without much effort, actually, and once I have it in my head – I carry poems around in my head, I don't write them down for days and I can recite them from my head – I can do it, and it seems quite easy, but the other kind requires a lot of work, searching for new sounds, new ideas, cross sections.[12]

He was also conscious of the different kind of demands they made on readers: 'When I have read those poems I feel that in fact there's nothing going across, because people are listening to completely new forms to which they've had no kind of introduction at all. [...] You can see the complete look of bewilderment.'[13] Compositionally, this type of writing meant cutting down a poem, compressing the language until a shape emerged:

> What you're getting in fact was the facets of a diamond [... The poems] were dealing with shape directly. I'd never dealt with shape before, in fact what I'd dealt with was content. What you've got is not the background to the poem – in fact most poems are the background to what really should be said – what you've got is the high force energy, the compressed centre.[14]

The pauses that, in *Brother Wolf*, suspended an ongoing rhythm, a rhythm moulded by grammar and meaning (even though pushed to the edge of breakdown), now become integral to shape. The poem is not carved out of a block of time, but stands alone, held up, in Mottram's phrase, by its 'symmetrizing spine'. That is to say, all components of shape (sound, syntax, semantics, typography) are placed on a single plane: this is the 'symmetry'. And the fact that language is expenditure of time-energy is exposed, instead of being hidden behind meaning: as Steve McCaffery puts it, a 'graphic, phonic or gestural materiality [of language] that is a necessary condition of, yet unsubsumable to, the ideality of meaning'.[15]

There is a randomness about the selection of words in the *Odes*. Selection, in linguistics, is the choosing of one word out of the network which the language offers, in order to suit a particular topic; for example the word 'mottled', out of a range of synonyms and antonyms which would include dappled, blotchy, pied, black, white, not to mention somewhat more distant relatives like pitted and smooth which are drawn in via the implication of a surface. But in a poem like 'Beak Ode' what does 'Cave/ rime' have to do with the red and blue 'filters' or 'mottled death' which precede and follow it? There is no 'topic' which would make sense of the selection of these words.[16] Not that selection of words ceases; rather, the tension between shape and randomness is pushed to an extreme. The writing places a huge torque upon the axis of selection, which in turn tends to become the vertical axis of the poem, especially when formed of single words, as happens in nine of the eighteen lines of 'Beak Ode'.

Physical gesture and the shape of the poems on the page interconnect. Take 'Lash Ode':

>   I put my walking stick
>   inside.
>   Its steel tip runs, towards
>   her cashmere
>   breast.
>
>   Wax her.
>   Shame the day.
>   Blame lizards
>   for the iguana rain.
>
>   Leverets.
>
>   Fences
>   & phones.
>
>   Apples ground
>   in mills
>   are red
>   and green.
>
>   How much you mean
>   to others,
>   more to me. Pods

>   that glaze
>   snap open tiny
>
>   bulbs who eat
>   my stem
>   towards the sky.
>   Cirrus.

(WT 53)

The starting point is a gesture of domination, the object flesh, its penetrated softness imaged in fashion magazine clothing fetishism, orthodox sadism ('wax' suggests whacks, the fixed image hides violence): a particular theatre of desire. After that the poem moves more abstractly: probing how the act of blaming animal nature relates to disavowing animal tenderness ('Leverets'), probing the relation without introducing an idea of it, because the abstractions the poem works with are concrete, not conceptual. The seething detail has been cut away, not suppressed, and continues to be implicated.

How words grasp that seething is written into the form of the poem. On the plane of content, the poem seeks out the mediations by which the materials have been formed: industrial ones ('Fences', 'phones', 'mills'), biological ones ('Pods', 'bulbs' 'stem'), and those of desire ('How much you mean/ to others,/ more to me'). The latter runs through all the others. But there's no comforting myth of human desire expressed by nature (the tradition of occidental love poetry). Instead, there are 'bulbs who eat/ my stem': nature feeding on us.[17] What is the relation between this and sadomasochistic desire? Perhaps what they share is waste. 'TO WASTE IS TO LIVE THE EXPERIENCE OF WEALTH,'[18] where desiring is to waste, and the human in nature is to be wasted.

To describe this type of compressed composition, MacSweeney used the word 'nodal', implying knotting and tight weaving. 'Node' is a term that Pound used to describe the poetic image in his early formulations of Modernist poetics. As Hugh Kenner explains, a knot is a form that energy rushes through, so that the human body is also a knot or series of knots.[19] But there are key differences between Pound and MacSweeney which mark the latter as a late Modernist. Pound in 1914 wrote of the image as 'a radiant node or cluster' and later added the statement 'energy creates pattern'. In Pound's own practice as a poet these principles translate into a method of 'luminous detail', where facets of objects are gathered into a field of simultaneous perceptions and worked into a continuous surface.[20] 'Brother Wolf' had begun to break with those principles: Chatterton's body takes different shapes, blood in water or staircase for fish, that are strongly disjunctive. There is no consistent surface of visual images. With the *Odes*, the discontinuities are more forceful, more extreme. Take 'Real Ode', which begins by setting a recognizable scene, but then moves into strong disjunction:

>   Wedding rings & tears. You are on
>   the edge of nowhere, next
>   to a moat.
>   [...]
>
>   Tangerine
>   frock
>   hugs pleated
>   folds
>   to
>   restless
>   body
>   Rim.
>
>   Happy then.
>   Smiled.
>
>   'I can't see
>   to finish this'
>
>   Right.
>
>   Conifer
>   &
>   Carp.
>
>   Swan.
>
>   Ghastly
>   sight.

(*WT* 63)

The details are certainly not 'luminous'; though some might belong to an English country house location (moat, conifer, carp, swan) they do not add up to a montage of 'shots' as in a film, which is one way of describing Pound's method in the *Cantos*. In other words no continuous, sutured surface forms in a reader's imagination. The erotically fascinating surface of the 'Tangerine/ frock' encloses like a rim a 'restless body', but the other meaning of rim, '(lick or suck) a person's anus', breaks that brief continuity, while it turns from noun to imperative verb (do this), suddenly changing the momentum.[21] It is not an easy ride; there is something painful – lacerating – about the form itself, such that the column of isolate words, from 'Right' to 'Swan', hurts. A scene is sparsely but sharply indicated: a wedding which is also a separation: they are the same thing. Such is the degree of condensation, and pain. Only occasionally does a stretch of narrative come in, to give relief. The poem is not an act of confession. This is somebody run through by nature and language.

This poem tracks the displacements that happen before there can be such a thing as a self or subject, as with:

> Moat bank saplings
> tilt
> for the sun
>
> Their roots
> push down.
>
> Drought
> &
> Flood.
>
> It's in the
> human blood
>
> Now cry.
>
> (*WT* 64)

If 'tilt' brings in tourneys (the castle theme), the other meaning – to waver from the vertical – pulls the eye in, dizzy and close to the ground rather than surveying from above. This is not the reassuring eighteenth-century Walpolish Nature that behaves like a gentleman, but something wild and strange that traverses us – the real is wild, includes death – it's *that* sobering. This is not a moral lesson (learn from nature, to be stoical), but pain inside word and image, their common axis.

The *Odes* do not give us images, in the traditional sense. They recall Rimbaud's method, in *Illuminations*, which is a magic lantern show of jostling scenes, ordered by their intensities rather than by spatial logic.[22] But the difference is that these poems do not give us a continuous play of the visual; they plunge suddenly through other dimensions, 'cutting across meaning' even more violently than Rimbaud. One of MacSweeney's own comments was that the poems are 'shocking'.[23] Certainly, there is a feeling of physical shock about them, and this is related to the use of language as a spell, a compulsion. A spell has nothing to do with the ordinary idea of meaning, in which messages are exchanged between speakers and listeners. That idea of expression makes the assumption that the forms of expression – images and rhetoric – are more or less transparent. But if words work like a spell, then their meaning in the ordinary sense is of secondary importance, because what matters is their effect on another body. The words themselves start to act like substances, as in an alchemic formula, or spells used by witches and shamans, as in 'Ode: Resolution':

> Pass the aconite.
> Wear monk's hood
> ringed with
> wolf bane.
>
> (*WT* 56)

Aconite, monk's hood, and wolf bane are names of poisonous substances, linked with a long tradition of herbal potions. Aconite, for example, was reputed to be 'of such force, that if a man especially, and then next any foure footed beast be wounded with an arrow or other instrument dipped in the juyce thereof, they die within halfe an houre after remidilesse'.[24] When language acts like a spell, then to name the substance is to be in contact with its effects. That experience of meaning only survives, watered down, in fantasy literature – watered down and hived off into a territory called 'magic', whereas it used to be, until less than two hundred years ago, part of the everyday English language. This poem is once again about Chatterton, and the history of the language:

> French words dominated
> Chaucer's day.
>   They ate away
> the oak & rose.

Most linguistic theory would not swallow the claim that things could be so affected. But this is poetry and it is claiming that things themselves were diminished by changes in the language. The words affect the things, the things exist inside the words.[25]

But to choose northern English had its cost:

> Chatterton knew
>   his way to a
>   northern
>   Cup. That kind
> of final act
>   is difficult
> to follow.

Yet why an equivalence between poetry and death? As well as a death chosen, as with Christian symbolism, 'Cup' rhymes with the poisonous substances, along the axis of language as spell, operating as laceration and shock:

> Watch yr breath.
> It will lie
> to you then lie
>   down and stop.

Too close to death for normal speech, this is the explosive ambiguity of black humour, making suicide a defiant act against all submission, even to death. The chain of submissions stretches back to the gentry who owned culture, and forward to their twentieth-century epigones ('He lay down// & was Recognised/ in romantic oils'). The whole book is haunted by suicide and early death, in the persons of Jim Morrison and Thomas Chatterton especially, as a deep ambiguity: a self-destruction but also a rebellious act that preserves life against deadness, in which the poet, in Mottram's phrase, is 'the vitalizer of language'.[26] MacSweeney had written this in *Elegy for January*:

> Thomas, what is there, after all, after youth. All these poems dedicated to you, written by poets past their teens. Our resilient

animal instinctiveness fails us, with age – we cannot hunt any longer, but lag behind for scraps. Only youth can mark the essential path across the world, of people, love, and language.

Can we allow ourselves to grow neatly into bigotry? Is that, too, a necessary portion of our making? Then it is better to be unnatural. (I think of the motorcyclist who does not attempt to avoid the head-on crash, but accelerates into his death.) *We must finish while ascending, and never come back.*

Here is the suicide imperative at its most naked:

> Quit
> now.
> Cascade your promises
> like unfulfilled
> stars.
>
> (*WT* 57)

The imperatives ('Quit', 'Cascade your promises') take away the power of calendar time, replace it with a 'now' of wastage ('Fill what's there/ with gelded/ heifer-blood'). Instead of the death instinct, as mere release from pain, a decision to embrace death: a thirst for riches. The enormous vitality of the poems can be seen as a flame that rises as it consumes.

'Wolf Tongue', subtitled 'a Chatterton Ode', includes many samples of Chatterton's more grainy words, such as 'Mie blodde steyned Veste', which clash with Horace Walpole's suave accumulation of culture: 'Walpole/ selling his shares in the future/ of english poetry' (*WT* 68), Walpole the Saatchi of his time. Those strong consonants that slow the tongue, in contrast to the smooth semantics of the southern English man of power, extend into MacSweeney's diction, as when he writes 'clonic/ twitching pride/ of lions suckt a death' (*WT* 69). The language is visceral. And that, for MacSweeney, is a question of how body becomes language: 'Panther, your/ jet body is a star'. As for Chatterton's body, 'Dorsiflexion/ writhed his feet/ into the living history/ of language', where 'dorsiflexion', highly consonantal, means bent or bowed backwards, for example of the spine. Or when it is the body of children, 'Crystal// children suckt/ life their ankles/ snapped into a wilderness/ of speech' (*WT* 70). The body in torsion, broken or dispersed, is the cost of giving life to the language: 'no man so potent/ breathes to vitalise/ the language of his day' (*WT* 71). MacSweeney used the title of this poem, which is a manifesto of life against death in language, for the collection that he prepared before his death, published by Bloodaxe in 2003.

The poem 'Wolf Tongue', like MacSweeney's work as a whole, is not made up of one language but many; it speaks in different tongues. The poet throws languages against each other and stays in the turbulent place where they meet. Smooth and pitted languages push against each other. 'I learned in Florence how to poison flowers': this is Renaissance Italian become long English vowels, making a rounded and flowing sound, as against the 'rural *rrr*' of Northumberland, the 'lips inside an acorne-coppe' (*WT* 70). The differences could be classified as Latinate versus Anglo-Saxon respectively. But they are multiple and move in different dimensions. The first is airy and smoother, the second sticky and slower, dense in its physicality. Part of the trajectory of the first is towards Rimbaud, 'French in the dark', language as illumination, light-source. The second is more corporeal, but the body it projects is twisted, broken, and in pain. The collision of languages is no simple binary, with good on one side and bad on the other.

Some of the complexity is given in the following:

> to run is
> limed fire, eat
> motion
> with rust.
>
> (*WT* 72)

If 'run' assembles meanings of quick bodily motion and flowing liquid, both of which relate in different ways to 'fire', 'limed', on the other hand, means muddied, sticky, capable of trapping, and yet it is a Latin-derived word. Unencumbered speed and stickiness; smooth and pitted surface; swift movement and invisibly slow corrosion cross from side to side of the divide and make new divisions. 'They cool to blood/ the tungsten carpet/ of my tongue' places smooth tongue and rough tongue, flesh and hard metal, in a non-fixed relationship of interpenetration, and, picking up an earlier reference to Chatterton's blood dispersed into the River Severn, make death the cost of the smooth tongue. Smooth and rough echo Dante's recommendation of rough words in his treatise *De Vulgari Eloquentia*, a piece of advice congruent with MacSweeney's use of northern speech and working-class inflexions.

So the contrasts are of specific surfaces and movements, and the particular uses of the body and its tongue which they relate to. Speakers are inside the language and cannot plot its borders without using it: 'An absolute commitment/ to a language going north/ without maps' is a decision the poem emphasizes, yet it speaks of a suspension of semantic certainty (no maps) which is characteristic of an in-between zone, an edge where fragments fly off. Take the beginning of section 3:

>   whanne from his lyfe-bloode
>   rodde lemes
>   were fed.
>
>   berten
>   Neders
>
>   flashed across a fen
>   of sky blood, no man so potent
>   breathes to vitalise
>   the language in his day.
>
>   (WT 71)

The 'language going north' also needs the southern flat landscape, sky-like as fens are, for speed and expanse; blood is part of that surface, that book, blood of his death.

But can poetic language, however potent, compete against what has dominated the communication scene since 1950, the media event, and its later mutation, the hyper-real? MacSweeney's 'Jury Vet', written between 1979 and 1981, risks full submersion in the fast erotics of fashion: 'CHARTREUSE blanquette, shirt lavender, frayed/ mustard thongs. Brown heels on JOSE/ Blue heels on JANE' (WT 107). The narrative of this event is Vogue / fashion show style but the implication is that style in that sense has become the language of reality. However, the poem has no alternative language to propose. It exposes the entanglement of its own desire in nets of SM: 'Love bossette,/ hear my low prayer.// HEAR MY VERY LOW PRAYER.// Burn the venom from this heart' (WT 104). Refusing a voice of moral superiority, the poem displays desires for submission, normally too shameful to own.

Its real concern is power. But instead of criticizing the conduct of rulers, the poem goes for the deeper question, how power is produced, and does that by probing how the desire for the erotic fetish comes into being, who is its subject. A reader is enmeshed in the desiring machine as it assembles itself, its components the glistening appurtenances of fashion become flesh: an erotic body that embodies the gaze of power – what you are looking at is yourself-in-subjection. By entering right there, the poem risks losing itself in the endless proliferation of objects of desire, secret of consumerism. Its tactic is to take them and write *with* them, in 'TOTAL SIGNATURE': 'CERISE DRAGONETTE I have piled my heart./ Cherry blouse I will undo. [...] I am with you in/ TOTAL SIGNATURE' (*WT* 102).

Putting on consumer fetishism the writer exults in compulsive rhythms and low rhymes, later a trademark of rap ('let me chew all of your Shoes' (*WT* 101)), and uses punk techniques to plumb abject sex: 'take the mould, pube lichen, pistol come, quim/ trigger fanny juice, dewy fern/ hair swifted, sex weaponry/ in her go root' (*WT* 105). But unlike punk there is no show of abandoning the ideal: 'YOU THE SHIMMERTEXING PEARL/ WITHOUTEN SPOT OF BODY BRUISE', here echoing the medieval poem *Pearl* in full collision with mass-market fabrication ('tex', a favourite brand name in the cloth trade, from the Latin root for weaving, as in 'text'). In other words, the poem is willing to inhabit the hyper-real and to press, from inside, against the way it captures desire.[27] What gets exposed is the command to 'Be/ SIGNIFICANT': submit to the meaning-machine, otherwise you won't be there.

Through yieldingness and not through superiority, the poem comes through the fetish to the desire inside it, to 'SHE peewit. Peewee. Plover glove flame', to '*her ankles of fire*' (*WT* 105, 109). It moves from visual and tactile fascination to intensities without image, without any need for pink as signature of the feminine:

No pink clues
as
fuck seeds
dance
&
rage.

(*WT* 103)

This is the exit: desire without meaning. And, instead of the traditional lyrical image which 'stops time', time inside the

word. Time is the basic substance of exploitation: behind money is time.[28] But the ecstatic time of the poem cannot be accumulated, only spent. The Walpoles cannot get their hands on it. The problem is the whole meaning-system: no change without transformation of (the) language.
Intellectual control is not an option:

> I kissed my Errors as they came.
> Sucked sick real.
> Tears flowing on the bastard zero ground.
>
> (WT 112)

This is very close in, without the analytic distance that makes experience into detachable aspects. The writing is located on the same plane as reality, in other words at the level of its production, which includes the accelerated mood-changes of the media environment ('Snap, cool down, wind-up furnace/ nights, chewed' (WT 112)); its state of constantly excited desire ('If I cannot do it Now I'll do it/ with Someone Else'); its sadomasochistic logic ('Albion, your women wearing shoes./ Straps & thongs' (WT 111)). The word 'SPASTIC' (WT 113), surrounded by blank space, sums up much of this, with its meanings of involuntary contraction, damage, insult. The writing moves in exactly there, to the site of damage, to recuperate language as overflowing desire, precisely where meaning subordinates language to paralysed, jerking bodies, with

> Neck chains.
> Blot
> love
> come
> now.
>
> (WT 113)

Are these blots or dots ('Fuck dots/ grab the scene'), semen-stains jerked out of the captive body? Or do they sabotage the meaning-machine? 'Your single body's a striking SOVIET!' (WT 119)

The struggle entails journalism, the tabloid 'reality studios', as William Burroughs called them: 'kiss each nasty limpridden/ edition/ of the Real' (WT 114), where 'kiss' is erotic seeing and touching which can make the beholder 'crippled', in 'DOCILE ADJUSTMENT TO DAILY HORROR', in which the second phrase is, blackly, both the name of the newspaper and the reality, making voyeuristic anxiety-pleasure, as reality TV does. Tabloid headlines ('LOVEDOLE BEANOS' (*WT* 118)) offer readers enjoyment of a language loaded with resentment. The general proposal is these were necessary conditions for the coming to power of Margaret Thatcher, who is perhaps the subject of 'HER DEMOCRATIC RATHOLE MOUTH DELIGHTS THE GUESTS// & DRIVES// THEIR SECRET MUSIK SPARE' (*WT* 115).

Jury Vet exposes the synergy of state, law, media, and politicians. It exposes the 'YOU' action by which agencies of power address people and turn them into parts of the assemblage: 'Sun/ says Yes I Love You, But/ Don't Be Bright' (*WT* 115), where the Sun is the tabloid but also, grotesquely, our Star. MacSweeney takes that 'You' and turns it around: 'in vivid gutters made by YOU' (*WT* 125), '&/ I/ mean You' (*WT* 123). The 'You' now accuses readers of complicity. It is hard to think of a response to the post-1960s counter-revolution in Britain that goes further than *Jury Vet*. More than simply criticizing power, it tears the veil of language.

Jury Vet does not play an ideal lyrical language against actual degradation, the ideal freedom of nature against social bondage, as happens in the romantic tradition, say with Shelley's 'Ode to the West Wind'. Instead, it sings from within degradation, against it. *The Book of Demons* (1997) also confronts abjection, in this case that of alcoholism, but what has changed is the communicative action. The first poem ('Ode to Beauty Strength and Joy And In Memory of the Demons') presents alcoholic delirium with terrible clarity:

> This demon, this gem-hard
> hearted agent of my worst nightmare [...]
> this orchestrator of ultimate hatred,
> the man with no eyes, no cranium, no brow no hair.
> He will always be known as the Demon with the mouth of Rustling
> Knives, and the meshing and unmeshing blades
> are right in your face. The blades say: there are your
> bags. Pack them and come with us. Bring your bottles
> and leave her. The contract is: you drink, we don't.
>
> (*WT* 218)

It is curious that the demons deliver their ultimatum in a pared-down language which recalls that of the *Odes*, whereas the poet has given himself very long sentences that take a long time to finish. The long lines use a great deal of repetition and alliteration: 'in goldleaf of fallen nature already so readily ready for the rising/ sap of a dearest darling spring when we will start again' (*WT* 219). The insistent yearning takes us to the edge and brink of something else: other possibilities of life and history.

The historical ones are condensed into 'the greatest revolutionary poster that/ ever lived: the Suprematist Heart'. The book's presiding hero is not Jim Morrison but Kasimir Malevich, inventor of Suprematism during the period of Russian revolutionary ferment. After the 1917 revolution, Malevich became a resolute activist, placing his art at the disposal of social transformation. MacSweeney's book desires that protagonism ('I yearned for 200-point Cyrillic caps/ across seven cols or in cirrus strands' (*WT* 238)), but the Suprematist rethinking of public monuments is killed dead ('in a pullet neck-breaking snap') by the demons, who pervert the revolutionary poster as their client 'straps on his monumental thirst' (*WT* 218). The Suprematist transformation that MacSweeney's protagonist longs for would turn the book's yearning form of expression – does turn it when pathos becomes passion – into magnificence: 'The truly great span of the legs above the city, spread/ and wide, rodded north and south and electrified by power passing/ through beneath the novas and planets and starres. Magnetised!' (*WT* 219).

To acknowledge a 'Shattered Socialist Heart' does not mean becoming 'a replicant Labour Party goon'. Once again, MacSweeney takes on the paralysing and largely unspoken political shame of our time. The degeneration of language is part of that shame. And degeneration is one of the things that his vulgar-rhymed alliterative phrases register:

> Not to be out in rainy Nevsky Prospekt
> but here I am at the back of nowhere
>
> under a fickle sickle harvest five-year
> plan pearly Shirley shiny moon
>
> (*WT* 238)

Instead of revolutionary Russia with its emblem of hammer and sickle, a mucked-up emblem (Shirley Williams being one of the Labour 'deserters' who formed the Social Democrat Party), whose cheap rhymes signal the language of populist politics.

The book locates its own struggle with the degradation of language through some key examples: that of the Ranters and other radicals of the seventeenth century suppressed by the Walpoles; that of early revolutionary Russia put down by Stalinism; that of rock music of the late sixties, whose destruction is denounced by British Punk. Without the struggle for magnificence, only soap-opera populism is left.

The poems take soap-opera sentiment and break it against the realities it covers over. 'Daddy Wants To Murder Me' places the story of how the father destroyed the 7-year-old's poems and crushed the small boy's pride, beside a visit as alcoholic adult to the Durham Family Practitioner Committee. The poem loops back and forth several times, testing the damage of each moment against the other. What actually was said on each occasion is held in suspense. We are brought to the realization that the real violence resides in the language itself: a damage that remains and repeats in the language. The triple scenario, childhood, present, and the war zones of Northern Ireland takes the damage to its sources. The words not said are those of the father and the doctor: they come from the place of power.

Beyond the family, the book tracks violence to the state:

> Nailbite squall-stirring helicopter gunships
> of darkest green – it is dark now along the
> moonless river and dark and always dark –
> descend to drop the flogging hammers in.

(*WT* 240)

Is this to be read as making self-destruction and state terror equivalent? That surely would be a projection of self-pity. Yet the writing has moved beyond pity, to a past/future time, where death has already occurred: 'it is dark now [...] and always dark'. From there the unthinkable alliance can be heard: what links the helicopters with, in Dylan Thomas's phrase, 'the dying of the light'. And there comes a type of demented calm: 'it will be dark along the river and always// dark and Othello will pad freely demented/ a panther in my sickened heart'. From this other side of death, all is lost and all exists in its fullest richness:

> The emerging lanceheads of the chives are so
> beautiful tonight, by offshore rigs, mainland
> bridges and cranes, and humans walk beneath
> the stars by the streaming dark water where
>
> in the land of tumblestones it is dark and always
> dark. Hear the roots of the flowers stress even
> the mighty earth and cry.
>
> (WT 241)

The 'land of tumblestones' is the territory of *Pearl*, which prefaces *The Book of Demons* in the Bloodaxe publication, but which MacSweeney wrote in the middle of the *Demons* sequence and continued to add to after the book was published. The person named Pearl, as MacSweeney used to explain when presenting the poems at readings, is a childhood friend, aged between 5 and 6½ when they used to play together at Sparty Lea. Pearl is mute, because of a congenital cleft palate, and her companion, Bar (i.e. Barry), teaches her to write. The writer becomes Pearl, in a crossover of times and persons. This happens through the use of a voice which is hers but not hers, since she could not speak but strained to write on 'a grey roofslate' taught by the other. The two processes, the writing of the poems and writing as something discovered in childhood, come together, shaping the book's work with and upon language. The discovery of the Word through writing ('Even writing the words *rose* and *garment/* broke my heart; their real variousnesses/ pricked me awake when I expected it least' (WT 251)) occurs in constant mutual exchange with the children's discovery of their environment and their feelings.

To renew language by returning to the source is this book's strong desire. In 'Brother Wolf' that was not possible: 'Chatterton knew/ you may not return to the source/ when you're/ it and/ died' (WT 25). What makes it possible in *Pearl*? Certainly not nostalgia: this is not a sentimental return, a regret for what is lost. It is a book which refuses pity: 'Pity? Put it in the slurry with the rest of your woes./ I am Pearl, queen of the dale' (WT 197). This is not the past 'revisited' but the past freed from bondage to time, its possibilities released. Hence the relationship with Suprematism: 'The aim is victory over the sunne and to stand in a high place/ holding a red flag' finds its equivalences with 'We seized the sky and made it ours, spelling/ out the vapour trails' (*WT* 277, 278): writing as assault on the impossible. But where, inside the language as it stands and within socially available communication, can that be done from?

The writing grapples with that question by reshaping the places and instruments of meaning: writing, the voice, the book, and their various histories and contexts. Language, in the form of existing public communication, has been 'poisoned to a wreckage' by dumbing down in 'terrible tabloidations' (*WT* 196). Nor are left intellectuals any use; their claim to be the owners of correct meanings and forms of expression is equally vitiating:

> O paranoid Marxist Cambridge prefects,
> self-appointed guarantors of consonants and vowels
> and arrangement of everyday sentences, placing
> of punctuation marks, with which Pearl
> wished to be in steady flux, she said
> with fingers, eyes, thumbs and palms. Listen.
>
> (*WT* 196)[29]

The poem moves at this point beyond Pearl's voice, which had begun by addressing readers ('Listen, hark, attend ... '), towards resources which she did not have at her disposal and which the poem itself lays claim to. Her writing ('Permit me to say this on a grey roofslate, as I protect/ my poor writing, I can't do joined up, with soaked forearm/ from the driving rain') does not express her voice, since she can't speak. By disconnecting writing from voice in this way, the poem releases it from being a secondary replica of speech, a subordination which has held it in thrall in Western cultures, and returns it to a condition of free interchange with all the ways in which human beings make sense of environment. These include gestures of hands and face, which are Pearl's 'punctuation marks', her punctuation of the flow of experience, which is the beginning of meaning: punctuation as the hinge between shapeless flow and meaning, as immersion in the world and not as fastidious pedantic control.[30] Seeing, hearing, touching, smelling a whole environment and learning to recognize its details and move through it physically: learning to write and this other learning are placed flush with each other ('said all I could/ while heifers moaned in the stalls, clopping/ of hooves my steaming, shitting/ beast accompaniment'). This is not a romantic delusion but a theory of writing, similar to Derrida's critique of the subordination of writing to the voice, but richly exemplified by MacSweeney's creation of a place where the necessary disconnections and reconnections can begin actually to be made:

> Now I will circle and uncircle
> my index fingers forever alone
> in the pools, spelling and unspelling
> our tragic consequences.
>
> (WT 213)

The place of regeneration crucially depends upon the book as physical and spiritual object, re-imagined in contexts which are both ancient and late modern:

> though
> my screen is blank and charmless to the human core
> I have an unbending desire to marry consonants and vowels
> and mate them together
> in what you call phrases and sentences
> which can become – imagine it – books!
> I'd like to sit down with Stephen, inside the borage groves, sing him
> my songs of the stream.
> But of course I cannot.
> [...]
> All the skies are leased anyway. Nothing is owned
> by humans. It is an illusion nightmare.
> You fall through the universe
> clinging to unravelled knots and breaking strings.
>
> (WT 204)

From language as song to string theory, the book of the future will have to measure up to that. And it will have to confront the destruction of space and the damage to language in our time. The deeper you dig into *Pearl*, the harder its message. Nothing less than a full return to the sources of damage will do.

Pearl takes the voice back to gestures and signs written by the body: 'Pearl said: a-a-a-a-a-, pointing with perfectly poised/ index finger towards the rusty coloured dry stone wall' (WT 201). The effect is to stop language in its tracks, to stop the dull roar of interpretation machines (classrooms, newspapers, TV) and deliver us into a strange but familiar pain and silence:

> My hands are in the clouds again, thumping the sun.
> And then I would be a wild, not mild, child,
> stamping my feet and cry, cry, cry,
> looking up at the mesmeric flicker of adult mouths
> as they said A and E and I and U and O, all joined up
> in terrible tresses, looking down at me
>
> (WT 213)

A strange fade-out happens: the mouths are there, opening and closing, the sounds come out, get joined up, but there is no meaning, no weaving of a world, only 'terrible tresses'. It is poetry that is missing, yet already there, in Pearl's desire to write: Rimbaud's vowels, Milton's 'Golden-tressed Sun'. The child's entry into language is the source, the emergent future.

> The aim is victory over the sunne and to stand in a high place
> holding a red flag
> ready to lead unforgiven workers to righteous triumph.
> You must execute kings and adulterous princes
> and reserve the right to burn down Parliament.
> Fight for your rights for the rest of your days.
>
> (WT 277)

Notes

INTRODUCTION

1. Alan Sinfield, *Literature, Politics and Culture in Postwar Britain* (Oxford: Blackwell, 1989), 166.
2. Jeff Nuttall, *Bomb Culture* (London: MacGibbon and Kee, 1968), 95.
3. Quoted in Jeff Nuttall, *Bomb Culture*, 171.
4. For a view of the current situation, see Tony Trehy, *Text* (Bury: Bury Metropolitan Council, 2005).
5. Letter of 15 July 2006. He adds: 'Without doubt he was one of the strongest influences on me as I hit my writing stride in 1966.'
6. Iain Sinclair (ed.), *Conductors of Chaos* (London: Picador, 1996), 450.
7. Chris Torrance, letter of 15 July 2006.
8. Lee Harwood, *Collected Poems* (Exeter: Shearsman Books, 2004), 303.
9. Lee Harwood, *Collected Poems*, 299–300.
10. 'Lee Harwood and Eric Mottram: A Conversation', *Poetry Information*, 14 (1975–6), 4–18 (10).
11. Eric Mottram, 'The British Poetry Revival', in Robert Hampson and Peter Barry (eds), *New British Poetries: The Scope of the Possible* (Manchester: Manchester University Press, 1993), 15–50 (34).
12. Tom Leonard, 'The Locust Tree in Flower, and Why It Had Difficulty Flowering in Britain', *Poetry Information*, 16 (1976–7), 9–14.
13. Tom Raworth, *A Serial Biography* (London: Fulcrum Press, 1968), 27–8.
14. Barry MacSweeney, *Wolf Tongue* (Newcastle: Bloodaxe, 2003), 29.
15. Robert Duncan, *The Opening of the Field* (New York: New Directions, 1973), 7.
16. Many thanks to Phil Maillard for pointing this out.
17. Eric Mottram, 'Paul Evans, a Personal Memoir', in Peter Bailey and Lee Harwood (eds), *The Empty Hill: Memories and Praises of Paul Evans* (Brighton: Skylark Press, 1992), 66–70.
18. This phrase appears in Shelley's poem 'Mont Blanc': 'An unremitting interchange/ With the clear universe of things around.'

19. I am drawing here on the Argentinian novelist and poet Juan José Saer's preface to the work of Juan L. Ortiz, forthcoming from Fondo de Cultura Económica, Mexico City.

CHAPTER 1. LEE HARWOOD: EMBRACING UNCERTAINTY

1. 'Lee Harwood and Eric Mottram: A Conversation', *Poetry Information*, 14 (1975–6), 4–18 (6). The first of Harwood's magazines was *Night Scene*, and it was followed by *Night Train*, *Soho* (a bilingual English and French magazine), *Horde*, and *Tzarad*.
2. Lee Harwood, in *Contemporary Authors Autobiography Series* (Detroit: Gale Research, 1994), vol. 19, 135–53 (140).
3. Ibid., 142.
4. Ibid.
5. I have followed the text as printed in *The White Room* (London: Fulcrum Press, 1968). The text of *Collected Poems* gives 'He said', with an initial capital letter. Robert Creeley, in *Pieces*, makes similar unconventional use of punctuation.
6. Ashbery's statement first appeared as a sleeve note for *The White Room* and is printed as the foreword to Harwood's *Crossing the Frozen River: Selected Poems* (London: Paladin, 1988), 11.
7. Robert Sheppard, 'Lee Harwood and the Poetics of the Open Work', in *New British Poetries*, 216–33 (231).
8. The phrase is Wittgenstein's (*Tractatus*, 6.4311): 'Death is not an event in life: we do not live to experience death. [...] Our life has no end in just the way in which our visual field has no limits.'
9. *Tractatus*, 4.12 and 4.1212. The German word translated as 'represent' is *darstellen*, which means present, depict, and outline, as well as represent.
10. Ezra Pound, 'A Retrospect', in *Literary Essays of Ezra Pound*, ed. T. S. Eliot (London: Faber, 1954), 3–14 (3). '[William Carlos] Williams of course does this and [Charles] Reznikoff too,' as Harwood states in a letter of 23 March 2005.
11. Charles Olson and Robert Creeley, *The Complete Correspondence* (Santa Barbara: Black Sparrow, 1980), vol. 1, 79. Olson used Creeley's formulation in his famous essay on poetics, 'Projective Verse'. For a lively account of how American poets shook up the British scene, see Jeff Nuttall's *Bomb Culture*.
12. The characteristics of Harwood's reading are obviously hard to describe, and readers are referred to the Stream Records recording, parts of which are reproduced in the CD of Harwood's work released by Birkbeck College and Optic Nerve in the Rock Drill series and distributed by Carcanet.

13. Letter of 30 June 2006.
14. *Independent*, 13 August 2005, 10.
15. In Robert Hampson and Peter Barry (eds), *New British Poetries: The Scope of the Possible* (Manchester: Manchester University Press, 1993), 216–33.
16. 'Lee Harwood and Eric Mottram: A Conversation', 14.
17. Ibid., 12.
18. 'Before Schulz the Kiteman' is another poem that uses material from a comic, in this case the US comic strip *Pogo*, drawn by Walt Kelly.
19. Sheppard, 'Lee Harwood and the Poetics of the Open Work', 221.
20. Vesna Klein, MA dissertation on the poetry of Lee Harwood, Birkbeck College, 2002, 35.
21. Michael Joseph, 1968. Thanks to Lee Harwood for this information. Harwood writes, 'Wintle was an eccentric but real anarchic radical who was also one of the last British cavalry officers. He relentlessly fought for what he believed right no matter what the obstacles' (letter of 23 March 2005).
22. 'Lee Harwood and Eric Mottram: A Conversation', 11.
23. Michel de Certeau, *The Writing of History* (New York: Columbia, 1988), 19–49.
24. See Peter Middleton, 'The New Memoryism: How Computers Changed the Way We Read', *New Formations*, 50 (1993), 57–74 (69): 'poetry of memory strives for an authenticity capable of resisting the dissolution of identity'.
25. See William Carlos Williams, 'The Poem as Field of Action', in *Selected Essays* (New York: New Directions, 1969), 280–91; and Charles Olson, 'Projective Verse', in *Collected Prose* (Berkeley: University of California, 1997), 239–49.
26. Peter Middleton, 'Who Am I to Speak? The Politics of Subjectivity in Recent British Poetry', in Hampson and Barry, *New British Poetries*, 107–33 (108).
27. Quoted by Miriam Allott in her Introduction to *Matthew Arnold: Selected Poems and Prose* (London: Everyman, 1978), xxxviii–xxxix.
28. Ibid., 89.
29. Ibid., xxxix.
30. The first version of 'Cable Street' appeared in *POETMEAT*, no 7 (Christmas 1964–5). The editor, Dave Cunliffe, had suggested to Harwood that he write about the East End. The later version, published in *The White Room*, was edited and quite a lot was cut from that earlier version. There are a few further changes in the version that appears in *Collected Poems*.
31. T. S. Eliot's insistence that poetry could not handle the formless had become a guiding principle for the Movement.

32. See Ken Edwards, 'Grasping the Plural', in Denise Riley (ed.), *Poets on Writing: Britain 1970–1991* (London: Macmillan, 1992), 21–9. This essay was originally published with the title 'The We Expression', as a Reality Studios Occasional Paper. Hardt and Negri write: 'The political synthesis of social space is fixed in the space of communication [...] language, as it communicates [...] creates subjectivities, puts them in relation, and orders them' (Michael Hardt and Antonio Negri, *Empire* (Cambridge, MA: Harvard University Press, 2001), 33).
33. See Tom Leonard, 'The Locust Tree in Flower'.
34. Sheppard, 'Lee Harwood and the Poetics of the Open Work', 222.
35. 'Lee Harwood and Eric Mottram: A Conversation,' 11.
36. Ibid., 14.
37. Creeley's book of essays, *A Sense of Measure* (London: Calder, 1972), gives a useful account of his poetics in this respect.
38. 'Marriage as a Psychological Relationship', in Joseph Campbell (ed.), *The Portable Jung* (New York: Penguin, 1976), 163–77 (170).
39. 'Lee Harwood and Eric Mottram: A Conversation', 2.
40. See William Carlos Williams's 1948 essay, 'The Poem as Field of Action', in *Selected Essays* (New York: New Directions, 1969), 280–91; and Eric Mottram, 'Open Field Poetry', *Poetry Information*, 17 (1977), 3–23.
41. See Fredric Jameson, *The Prison House of Language* (Princeton: Princeton University Press, 1972), where he speaks of 'the illusory order of nouns and substances' as a product of language (p. 173).
42. *Captain Harwood's Log of Stern Statements and Stout Sayings* (London: Writers Forum, 1973), 13, quoting Gide.
43. Letter of 14 June 2002.
44. See below p. 106.

CHAPTER 2. CHRIS TORRANCE: LYRIC AND THE LARGER PROCESS

1. 'Chris Torrance, Interviewed by Peter Hodgkiss', *Poetry Information*, 18 (1977–8), 3–11 (3).
2. Blake wrote, in T*he Marriage of Heaven and Hell*, 'Energy is Eternal Delight.'
3. The reader is referred to William Carlos Williams's poem 'To Elsie', from *Spring and All* (1923): 'no-one to witness/ and adjust, no-one to drive the car'.
4. For Bataille, in his searing critique of progress, the aim of accumulating energy resources does not lead to autonomy, but to

subordinating oneself to the future. See Georges Bataille, *The Accursed Share* (New York: Zone Books, 1991), vol. 1, 190.
5. Keith Tuma, *Anthology of Twentieth-Century British and Irish Poetry* (New York: Oxford University Press, 2001), 22.
6. In Freud's account of the production of dream images, these emerge, like mushrooms out of the multiple and undifferentiated mycelium ('the mycelium brooding and waiting', as Torrance writes (*TH* 351)).
7. Chris Torrance, *Acrospirical Meanderings in a Tongue of the Time* (London: Albion Village Press, 1973). One of its dedicatees is Lee Harwood. Albion Village Press was run by Iain Sinclair.
8. Ordinary judgment has it that paranoia is pathological. Torrance's poem takes it as the real, as does Jack Kerouac in *Visions of Cody*. William Burroughs and Iain Sinclair have used paranoia as a method for discovering occulted realities.
9. Georges Bataille, *Visions of Excess* (Manchester: Manchester University Press, 1985), 82, 84.
10. Shapelessness is a characteristic of the body without organs: See Gilles Deleuze and Félix Guattari, *Anti-Oedipus: Capitalism and Schizophrenia* (Minneapolis: University of Minnesota, 1983), 8.
11. *The Collected Books of Jack Spicer* (Los Angeles: Black Sparrow, 1995), 25.
12. *Acrospirical Meanderings*, 37.
13. Bataille, *Visions of Excess*, 129.
14. References are given as *MD* followed by a numeral to indicate the book number. The books are: *The Magic Door* (*MD1*) (London: Albion Village Press, 1975); *Citrinas* (*MD2*) (London: Albion Village Press, 1977); *The Diary of Palug's Cat* (*MD3*) (Newcastle: Galloping Dog Press, 1980); *The Book of Brychan* (*MD4*) (Newcastle: Galloping Dog Press, 1982); *The Slim Book/Wet Pulp* (*MD5*) (Swansea: Stone Lantern Press, 1986); *Rori – A Book of the Boundaries* (1988, unpublished); *Southerly Vector/The Book of Heat* (Neath: Cwm Nedd Publications, n.d. [1996]); *Path* (in progress, partially published as *Wobbly Chair* (Cardiff: Canna Press, 2003)). The total is nine if *Southerly Vector/The Book of Heat* is taken as two books.
15. *The Collected Books of Jack Spicer*, 61.
16. Carl Jung, 'The Idea of Redemption in Alchemy', in *The Integration of the Personality* (London: Kegan Paul, 1940), 205–80 (208).
17. Phil Maillard, 'Chris Torrance: A Profile' (unpublished typescript), 6. Maillard's essay was published in abridged form as 'The Press of Performance and Debate', in *New Welsh Review*, 24 (1993), 52–3.
18. Jung, 'The Idea of Redemption in Alchemy', 256, 240.
19. Phil Maillard points out that 'regrettably, this was accidentally printed upside down in the book' (letter of 26 July 2006).

20. *I Ching* (London: Routledge, 1983), 16–17.
21. Iain Sinclair, 'Chris Torrance: A Fly-Sheet Homage', *Poetry Information*, 14 (1975–6), 19–22 (22).
22. Ibid., 21.
23. *The Collected Books of Jack Spicer*, 281, 183.
24. I am indebted to Phil Maillard's essay 'Chris Torrance: A Profile' for this information.
25. Maillard, 'Chris Torrance: A Profile', 4-5.

CHAPTER 3. BARRY MacSWEENEY: THE FIRE-CROWNED TERRAIN

1. Maggie O'Sullivan, review of Barry MacSweeney's *Ranter*, *Reality Studios*, 8 (1986), 83.
2. Nicholas Johnson, 'Barry MacSweeney, An Appreciation', *Pores*, 1 (www.pores.bbk.ac.uk/1/index.html).
3. Barry MacSweeney, *Elegy for January* (London: Menard Press, 1970), 23.
4. The quotation is from George Gregory's 'Life of Thomas Chatterton' (1789), reprinted as an introductory essay in Southey's edition of *The Works of Thomas Chatterton* (London: Longman, 1803), vol. 1, xxxvi. I am grateful to Michael Baron for this information.
5. Clive Bush, *Out of Dissent: A Study of Five Contemporary British Poets* (London: Talus Editions, 1977), 359–60; see also p. 347.
6. Basil Bunting, 'Some Limitations of English', in *Basil Bunting: Three Essays*, ed. Richard Caddell (Durham: Basil Bunting Poetry Centre, 1994), 22–6.
7. Emerald light is important in Sufi tradition. See Henri Corbin, *The Man of Light in Iranian Sufism* (New York: Omega, 1994), 43–8.
8. 'Barry MacSweeney Interviewed by Eric Mottram', *Poetry Information*, 18 (1977–8), 21–39 (37).
9. 'Barry MacSweeney Interviewed by Eric Mottram', 37.
10. See Paul Virilio, *Speed and Politics* (New York: Semiotext(e), 1986).
11. See Guy Debord, *The Society of the Spectacle* (New York: Zone Books, 1995), 114: 'Everything really lived has no relation to society's official version of irreversible time [...] Such individual lived experience of a cut-off everyday life remains bereft of language or concept.'
12. 'Barry MacSweeney Interviewed by Eric Mottram', 38.
13. Ibid., 37.
14. Ibid., 36.

15. Steve McCaffery, 'Writing as a General Economy', in *North of Intention* (New York: Roof Books, 2000), 201–21 (204).
16. Jakobson defines the poetic function as the projection of equivalence from the axis of selection onto the axis of combination, combination being uses of sound and rhythm. One of the problems of this definition, which generally works well with early Modernist writing, is that it is less suitable for later Modernist poetry, where selection is itself integral to form, as, say, in J. H. Prynne's work. See Roman Jakobson, 'Linguistics and Poetics', in David Lodge (ed.), *Modern Criticism and Theory: A Reader* (London: Longman, 1988), 32–57 (39).
17. See Marx's *Economic and Philosophical Manuscripts of 1844* (New York: International Publishers, 1971), 112: 'Man *lives* on nature – means that nature is his *body*, with which he must remain in continuous interchange if he is not to die. [...] An animal produces only itself, whilst man reproduces the whole of nature.' In MacSweeney's poem the relationship with nature is reversed, such that nature is the active agent: the world upside down, the world of fetishism. Yet his abstractions are concrete because human time (labour) runs through them. His work is thus a critique of fetishism.
18. McCaffery, 'Writing as a General Economy', 219.
19. Hugh Kenner, *The Pound Era* (London: Faber, 1975), 146.
20. See Marjorie Perloff, *Radical Artifice* (Chicago: University of Chicago Press, 1994), 55.
21. Pound's knots are, as Kenner observes, 'topologically stable': 'a patterned integrity accessible to the mind; topologically stable'; '"energy creates pattern." [...] particulars of the pattern mutate; the pattern is stable' (*The Pound Era*, 146–7). MacSweeney's knots are not stable.
22. Take, for example, the first section of 'Childhood': 'At the edge of the forest – the flowers of dream tinkle, explode, illuminate – the girl with orange lips, knees crossed in the clear downpour that deafens the fields, nakedness shaded, crossed, clothed by rainbows, the flora, the sea.'
23. 'Barry MacSweeney Interviewed by Eric Mottram', 37.
24. *Gerdlad's Herbal* (1636), cited by Mottram, 'Reading Barry MacSweeney's Odes', *Maxy's Journal*, 3 (1979), 28–39 (32).
25. For an elaboration of this idea, see Walter Benjamin, 'On Language as Such and On the Language of Man', in *Reflections* (New York: Schocken, 1986), 314–32 (316–17).
26. 'Reading Barry MacSweeney's *Odes*', 39.
27. MacSweeney brings Rimbaud's *Illuminations* into the twentieth century with phrases such as 'palaces/ of ULTRA REAL' (WT 114). See Rimbaud's poem 'Promontory Palace'.

28. See Karl Marx, *Grundrisse* (Harmondsworth: Penguin, 1973), 173: 'Economy of time, to this all economy ultimately reduces itself.'
29. The concerns are similar to those of Lee Harwood's 'Bathtime'; see above, p. 47.
30. See Gregory Bateson, 'The Logical Categories of Learning and Communication', in *Steps to an Ecology of Mind* (London: Paladin, 1973), 251–79.

Select Bibliography

LEE HARWOOD

Works

The White Room (London: Fulcrum Press, 1968).
Landscapes (London: Fulcrum Press, 1969).
The Sinking Colony (London: Fulcrum Press, 1970).
Penguin Modern Poets, 19, with John Ashbery and Tom Raworth (Harmondsworth: Penguin, 1971).
Captain Harwood's Log of Stern Statements and Stout Sayings (London: Writers Forum, 1973).
HMS Little Fox (London: Oasis Books, 1975).
All the Wrong Notes (Durham: Pig Press, 1981).
Crossing the Frozen River: Selected Poems (London: Paladin, 1988).
Morning Light (London: Slow Dancer Press, 1998).
Collected Poems (Exeter: Shearsman Books, 2004).

Biographical and Critical Studies

Harwood, Lee, *Contemporary Authors Autobiography Series* (Detroit: Gale Research, 1994), vol. 19, 135–53.
'Lee Harwood and Eric Mottram: A Conversation', *Poetry Information*, 14 (1975–6), 4–18.
Lopez, Tony, 'The White Room in the New York Schoolhouse', in *Meaning Performance* (Cambridge: Salt Publishing, 2006), 105–20.
Sheppard, Robert, 'Keeping the Doors Open: The Poetry of Lee Harwood in the 1960s and 1970s', in *The Poetry of Saying: British Poetry and its Discontents 1950–2000* (Liverpool: Liverpool University Press, 2005), 103–24.
—— (ed), *The Salt Companion to Lee Harwood* (Cambridge: Salt Publishing, 2007).
Skelt, Peterjon, 'Lee Harwood', in *Prospect into Breath: Interviews with North and South Writers* (London: North and South, 1991), 60–78.

Weatherhead, A. Kingsley, 'Lee Harwood', in *The British Dissonance: Essays on Ten Contemporary Poets* (Columbia, MO: University of Missouri Press, 1983), 173–91.

CHRIS TORRANCE

Works

Green, Orange, Purple, Red (London: Ferry Press, 1968).
Aries Under Saturn and Beyond (London: Ferry Press, 1969).
Acrospirical Meanderings in a Tongue of the Time: Poems, Glymercher Isaf, June 1970 to October 1972 (London: Albion Village Press, 1973).
The Magic Door, Book 1 (London: Albion Village Press, 1975).
Citrinas: The Magic Door, Book 2 (London: Albion Village Press, 1977).
The Diary of Palug's Cat: The Magic Door, Book 3 (Newcastle: Galloping Dog Press, 1980).
The Book of Brychan: The Magic Door, Book 4 (Newcastle: Galloping Dog Press, 1982).
The Slim Book / Wet Pulp: The Magic Door, Book 5 (Swansea: Stone Lantern Press, 1986).
The Tempers of Hazard, with Thomas A. Clark and Barry MacSweeney (London: Paladin, 1993).
Wobbly Chair (Cardiff: Canna Press, 2003).

Biographical and Critical Studies

Brinton, Ian, 'Black Mountain in England (2)', *PN Review*, 163 (2005), 74–7.
Freeman, John, review of *The Book of Brychan*, *Poetry Wales*, 18:4 (1983), repr. in *The Less Received* (Exeter: Stride, 2000), 54–9.
Hodgkiss, Peter, 'Chris Torrance, Interviewed by Peter Hodgkiss', *Poetry Information*, 18 (1977–8), 3–11.
Hool, Ric (ed.), *Wonderful Remark, a Celebration of Chris Torrance* (Blaina, Gwent: WYSIWYG Chapbooks, 2000).
Lopez, Tony, 'Sustainable Poetics', review of *The Tempers of Hazard*, *Parataxis*, 4 (1993), 86–8.
MacSweeney, Barry, 'An Enthusiasm', *Poetry Information*, 9/10 (1974), repr. in *The Tempers of Hazard* (London: Paladin, 1993), 325–6.
Maillard, Phil, 'The Press of Performance and Debate', *The New Welsh Review*, 24 (1993), 52–3.
—— 'A Celebration Took Place', *Global Tapestry Journal*, 24 (2001), 9–13.
Prynne, Jeremy, 'The Singing Voice…', *The Tempers of Hazard* (London: Paladin, 1993), 295–6.

Sinclair, Iain, 'Chris Torrance: A Fly-Sheet Homage', *Poetry Information*, 14 (1975–6), 19–2.

BARRY MACSWEENEY

Works

The Boy from the Green Cabaret Tells of His Mother (London: Hutchinson, 1968).
Brother Wolf (London: Turret Press, 1972).
Odes (London: Trigram Press, 1978).
Black Torch (London: New London Pride, 1978).
The Tempers of Hazard, with Thomas A. Clark and Chris Torrance (London: Paladin, 1993).
Pearl (Cambridge: Equipage, 1995).
The Book of Demons (Tarset, Northumberland: Bloodaxe, 1997).
Etruscan Reader, vol. 3, with Maggie O'Sullivan and David Gascoyne (Exeter: Etruscan Books, 1997).
Wolf Tongue: Selected Poems 1965–2000 (Newcastle: Bloodaxe, 2003).

Biographical and Critical Studies

Brinton, Ian, review of *Wolf Tongue*, *Tears in the Fence*, 37 (Spring 2004), 94–100.
Bush, Clive, 'Dance Hymns on a Semi-Stable Planet', in *Out of Dissent: A Study of Five Contemporary British Poets* (London: Talus Editions, 1997), 211–303.
Johnson, Nicholas, 'Barry MacSweeney, An Appreciation', *Pores*, 1 (www.pores.bbk.ac.uk/1/index.html)
Mottram, Eric, 'Barry MacSweeney Interviewed by Eric Mottram', *Poetry Information*, 18 (1977–8), 21–39.
—— 'Reading Barry MacSweeney's Odes', *Maxy's Journal*, 13 (1979), 28–39.
O'Sullivan, Maggie, review of *Ranter*, *Reality Studios*, 8 (1986), 83.
Rowe, William, 'State Secrets: Names and Fetishes in Barry MacSweeney's *Jury Vet*', in Tony Lopez and Anthony Caleshu (eds), *Poetry and Public Language* (Exeter: Shearsman Books, 2007), 225–37.
Wheale, N., 'Sweeno's Beano', review of *The Book of Demons*, *London Review of Books* (1 October 1998), 35.

THE BRITISH POETRY REVIVAL

Barry, Peter, *Poetry Wars: British Poetry of the 1970s and the Battle of Earls Court* (Cambridge: Salt Publishing, 2007).
Bush, Clive, *Out of Dissent: A Study of Five Contemporary British Poets* (London: Talus Editions, 1977).
Crozier, Andrew, 'Thrills and Frills: Poetry as Figures of Empirical Lyricism', in Alan Sinfield (ed.), *Society and Literature 1945–1970* (London: Routledge, 1983), 199–233.
Edwards, Ken, 'The Two Poetries', *Angelaki*, 5:1 (2000), 25–37.
Hampson, Robert, and Barry, Peter (eds), *New British Poetries: The Scope of the Possible* (Manchester: Manchester University Press, 1993).
Leonard, Tom, 'The Locust Tree in Flower, and Why It Had Difficulty Flowering in Britain', *Poetry Information*, 16 (1976–7).
Middleton, Peter, 'Anonymous Poetry', *Angelaki*, 5:1 (2000), 131–43.
Mottram, Eric, 'The British Poetry Revival', in Robert Hampson and Peter Barry (eds), *New British Poetries: The Scope of the Possible* (Manchester: Manchester University Press, 1993), 15–50.
——'Open Field Poetry', *Poetry Information*, 17 (1977), 3–23.
——'Beware of Imitations: Writers Forum Poets and British Poetry in the '60s', *Poetry Student*, 1 (1975), 6–7, 32–5.
Nuttall, Jeff, *Bomb Culture* (London: MacGibbon and Kee, 1968).
Raworth, Tom, *A Serial Biography* (London: Fulcrum Press, 1968).
Removed for Further Study: The Poetry of Tom Raworth, The Gig, 13–14 (2003).
Sheppard, Robert, *The Poetry of Saying: British Poetry and its Discontents 1950–2000* (Liverpool: Liverpool University Press, 2005).

Index

Abstract Expressionism, 17
Adams, Henry, 40
Allott, Miriam, 111
anti-fascist, 33
Apollinaire, Guillaume, 5, 80
Arnold, Matthew, 30, 31–2, 111
Ashbery, John, 11, 13, 15, 22, 110, 117
Auden, W. H., 6, 32, 33

Bacon, Francis, 40
Bailey, Peter, 109
Baron, Michael, 114
Barry, Peter, 109, 111, 120
Basho, Matsuo, 56
Bataille, Georges, 62, 67, 112–13
Bateson, Gregory, 116
Baudelaire, Charles, 33
Beat, 3, 5
Benjamin, Walter, 115
BEPC, 4
Betjeman, John, 50
Blake, William, 5, 10, 42, 51, 112
Blaser, Robin, 49
Borges, Jorge Luis, 11, 16–17
British Poetry Revival, The, 2, 8, 86, 109, 120

Browning, Robert, 6
Bunting, Basil, 6, 9, 43, 70, 79, 80, 85–6, 88, 114
Burroughs, William, 101, 113
Bush, Clive, 85, 114, 119, 120
Byron, Lord (George Gordon), 25

Caddell, Richard, 114
Campbell, Joseph, 112
capitalism, 80, 113
Carlos Williams, William, 5, 11, 30, 110, 111, 112
Cash, Johnny, 80
Chatterton, Thomas, 5, 81, 82–7, 93, 95–7, 98, 105, 114
Chaucer, Geoffrey, 82, 96
Churchill, Winston, 34
Clare, John, 5
Cobbing, Bob, 3, 11
Coleridge, Samuel Taylor, 25, 69
collage, 27, 34, 43, 52
Constable, John, 17
consumer society, 10, 86
Corbin, Henri, 114
Corso, Gregory, 50
Creeley, Robert, 22, 38, 79, 110, 112
Crozier, Andrew, 50, 120

INDEX

Cunliffe, Dave, 111

Dada, 2, 7
Dante, Alighieri, 98
de Certeau, Michel, 29, 111
Debord, Guy, 114
Deleuze, Gilles, 113
Derrida, Jacques, 107
di Prima, Diane, 5
Dickens, Charles, 7
Doors, The, 4, 9, 80
Dorn, Ed, 5
Duffy, Carol Ann, 25
Duncan, Robert, 8, 109

Edwards, Ken, 112, 120
Eisenstein, Sergei, 35
Eliot, T. S., 25, 30, 32, 110, 111
Evans, Paul, 9, 25, 109

Ferlinghetti, Lawrence, 50
Freud, Sigmund, 113

Gide, André, 11, 35, 112
Ginsberg, Allen, 5, 50
Godard, Jean-Luc, 27
Gregory, George, 114
Guattari, Félix, 113
Guest, Barbara, 64

Hall, John, 64
Hampson, Robert, 109, 111, 120
Hardt, Michael, 112
HARWOOD, LEE
  'A Poem for Writers', 4
  All the Wrong Notes, 4, 47
  'Animal Days', 28–9, 31
  'As your eyes are blue', 12
  'Bath–time', 47

'Before Schulz the Kiteman', 111
'Cable Street', 32, 34, 38, 40, 111
'Cambridge Marxists', 47
Captain Harwood's Log of Stern Statements and Stout Sayings, 112
Collected Poems (CP), 12, 13, 15, 18, 20, 23, 25, 28, 29, 30, 32, 33, 35, 36, 38, 39, 40, 41, 43, 44, 45, 46, 47, 48
Contemporary Authors Autobiography Series, vol.19, 110
Crossing the Frozen River: Selected Poems, 110
emotion, 26, 39–43
experience, 13, 14, 25, 33, 34, 38, 40, 41, 44, 45, 47
field, 13, 20, 30, 38, 41, 43
'Final Painting, The', 20, 21
'For Paul [Evans]/ Coming out of winter', 25
framing, 14, 15, 16, 17, 18, 19, 20, 24, 38
'Gorgeous – Yet Another Brighton Poem', 46
heterogeneity, 34, 38
Horde, 110
'House, The', 22
immanence, 40
immediacy, 14, 19, 27, 42
intellect, 40–2
interstitial space, 37
jazz, 22, 46
'Landscapes', 17
Landscapes LP, 22
language of power, 47–8

'Linen', 12, 25–7
Long Black Veil, The, 34–5, 37, 40–3
love, 19, 33, 37, 39, 40, 41, 43, 46
materiality, 24, 30, 35, 44, 46
memory, 17, 18, 30, 31, 37, 111
Morning Light, 46, 117
multiplicity, 6, 26, 35, 40, 42
Night Scene, 110
Night Train, 110
non–linearity, 35, 42
'Paint Box, The', 15–16
painting, 14–21, 23, 27
phase–change, 40–1
'Qasida', 43, 46
Qasida Island, 43
Sinking Colony, The, 25, 31, 117
Soho, 110
space/spatiality, 12–14, 17–19, 27, 36–7, 39, 45, 112
surface, 13–14, 17, 20–1, 42–4, 46, 84
time/temporality, 7, 14–20, 25, 29, 30–1, 35–6, 38–42, 45
transcendence, 30, 35, 40
Tzarad, 110
'White', 13, 17
White Room, The, 110–11, 117
Heraclitus, 58
Hodgkiss, Peter, 112
Hopkins, Gerard Manley, 59
Hughes, Ted, 4, 38

Ives, Charles, 47

Jagger, Mick, *See* Rolling Stones
Jakobson, Roman, 115
Jameson, Fredric, 112
Johnson, Nicholas, 80
Jones, Brian, *See* Rolling Stones
Jones, David, 70
Joseph, Michael, 111
Joyce, James, 35, 41
Jung, Carl, 39, 40, 71–2, 112–13

Kant, Immanuel, 41
Keats, John, 25, 31
Kelly, Walt, 111
Kenner, Hugh, 92, 115
Kerouac, Jack, 50, 113
Khlebnikov, Velimir, 5
Klein, Vesna, 28, 111
Kline, Franz, 27
Kyger, Joanne, 38

Larkin, Phillip, 4, 22, 31, 33, 50
Lenin, V. I., 34
Leonard, Tom, 5–6, 109, 112, 120
Locke, John, 85–6, 87
Lodge, David, 115

Macmillan, Harold, 31
MACSWEENEY, BARRY
animal, 82, 87, 89, 92, 97
'Beak Ode', 88–9, 91
Book of Demons, The, 81, 102, 105, 119

INDEX

Boy from the Green Cabaret Tells of His Mother, The, 80, 119
Brother Wolf, ix, 81, 82, 87, 90, 93, 105, 119
'Childhood', 115
'Daddy Wants To Murder Me', 104
damage, 101, 104, 107
degeneration, 103
discontinuity, 93
disjunction, 93
dissent, 80
'Elegy for January', 82
eyeballing, 84
fetishism, 92, 100, 115, 119
Jury Vet, 99, 102, 119
'Lash Ode', 91
'Last Bud, The', 81
late modernism, 92, 107
linear form, 88
lived time, 89
node/nodal, 92
'Ode: Resolution', 95
Odes, 9, 87–8, 89–92, 93, 95, 103, 115, 119
Pearl, 88, 100, 105–7, 119
power, 7, 81, 82, 97, 99, 100, 102, 104
'Real Ode', 93
sadism, 92
sadomasochism, 92, 101
shape, 83, 85, 88–91, 106
Tempers of Hazard, The (TH), 61, 64
unfocused gaze, 84
violence, 7, 86, 92, 104
'Wolf Tongue', 97–8
Wolf Tongue (WT), 81, 82, 83, 84, 85, 86, 87, 88, 92, 93, 94, 95, 97, 98, 99, 100, 101, 102, 103, 104, 105, 106, 107, 108

Maillard, Phil, 24, 72, 109, 113, 114, 118
Malevich, Kazimir, 17, 103
Mallarmé, Stéphane, 25, 27, 41
Marx, Karl, 115, 116
Marxism, 47, 106, 115
Materialism, 87
McCaffery, Steve, 90, 115
Middleton, Peter, 30, 111, 120
Milton, John, 80, 108
Modernism, 5, 21–2, 25, 32, 41, 43, 86, 92, 115
Monk, Thelonius, 9
montage, 9, 34–5, 94
Morrison, Jim, *See* Doors, The
Motion, Andrew, 22
Mottram, Eric, 1, 90, 96, 109, 110, 111, 112, 114, 115, 117, 119, 120
Movement, The, 22, 31, 33, 111
Multiculturalism, 34

Negri, Antonio, 112
New York School, The, 22
Newman, Barnet, 17
Nietzsche, Friedrich, 44
Nuttall, Jeff, 2, 109, 110, 120

O'Hara, Frank, 11, 22
O'Sullivan, Maggie, 80, 90, 114, 119
Olson, Charles, 5, 30, 53, 74, 110, 111
Open Field, 43, 50
Oppen, George, 11

Ortiz, Juan L., 110
Orwell, George, 87

Parallel Tradition, The, 4, 43
Parker, Charlie, 2, 9, 54
Perloff, Marjory, 115
Plato, 17
Poetry Society, The, 1
Poetry Review, 1
Postmodernism, 41, 89
Pound, Ezra, 11, 21, 22, 25, 35, 79, 86, 92–3, 94, 110, 115
Prynne, Jeremy, 50, 60, 70, 115, 118

Raworth, Tom, 5, 6, 109, 117, 120
Realism, 57
Reinhardt, Ad, 17
Resnais, Alain, 27
Reznikoff, Charles, 110
Riley, Denise, 112
Rilke, Rainer Maria, 35, 42, 115
Rimbaud, Arthur, 2, 5, 80, 87, 95, 98, 108, 115–16
Rivers, Larry, 27
Rolling Stones, 3, 81
Romanticism, 25, 41, 81, 86
Rothko, Mark, 17

Saer, Juan José, 110
Schwitters, Kurt, 2, 5
Shelley, Percy, 5, 10, 25, 31, 66, 80, 81, 83, 102, 109
Sheppard, Robert, 25, 28, 35, 110, 111, 112, 117, 120
Sinclair, Iain, 9, 73–4, 109, 113, 114, 119
Sinfield, Alan, 1, 4, 109, 120

Snyder, Gary, 50
Spicer, Jack, 49, 65, 70, 74, 113, 114
Stalinism, 104
Suprematism, 103, 105
Surrealism, 7

Thatcher, Margaret, 3, 48, 69, 87, 102
Thomas, Dylan, 7, 104
TORRANCE, CHRIS
  Acrospirical Meanderings in a Tongue of the Time, 4, 56, 61, 68, 70, 71, 73, 78, 113, 118
  alchemy/alchemical, 50, 68, 70, 71–2, 74–5
  'Aries', 65
  Aries Under Saturn and Beyond (*ASB*), 53–6, 118
  Blues, 53
  Book of Brychan: The Magic Door, (*MD4*), 77–9, 113
  'Bread & Wine', 53
  'Candlemistress, The', 67
  'Carshalton Poems', 49, 50, 69
  Citrinas: The Magic Door (*MD2*), 74–6, 113
  CND, 50
  colour, 51, 52, 61, 71
  'Day–by–Day Poem', 63
  Diary of Palug's Cat: The Magic Door, (*MD3*), 67, 76–7, 113
  discontinuity, 75
  English Intelligencer, The, 50
  everyday, 7, 48, 52–3, 63–4, 68, 71, 73, 78
  '(for Val', 54

INDEX

Green, Orange, Purple, Red (GOPR), 49–54, 69
'House of Stone, The', 72
landscape, 67
'Letter to Barry MacSweeney', 76
'Letter to Lee', 73
love, 51, 54, 55
'Love Poem', 55
Magic Door, The (MD1), 70–4, 113
'Mirages', 76
'Mushroom Fever', 68
New American Poetry, 1945–1960, The, 50
'New Territory, The', 56
ORIGINS–DIVERSIONS, 50
'Poem – Summer', 54
'Poem (for Lee Harwood)', 54
'Poem to the Three Laughing Sages', 62
randomness, 51–2, 55, 60, 61, 64
recognition, 52, 78
sky–gazing, 51
Slim Book/Wet Pulp: The Magic Door, (MD5), 71, 78–9, 113
'Spinning the Poem', 64

'Spirit of the May Days', 67
'Straight from Sleep', 65–6
'Subsidence Was Pulsatory, However', 75
surfeit, 51, 57, 68
Tempers of Hazard, The (TH), 56, 57, 58, 60, 62, 63, 65, 66, 67, 68, 69, 70, 113
transformation, 64, 68, 70–2, 74
typography, 53, 55
unfocused gaze, 84
Torrance, Val, 54, 67, 73
Trehy, Tony, 109
Truffaut, François, 27
Tuma, Keith, 113
Tzara, Tristan, 5, 7, 11

Valéry, Paul, 42, 58
Virilio, Paul, 114

Walpole, Horace, 84, 94, 97, 101, 104
Williams, Shirley, 104
Wintle, A.D., 29, 111
Wittgenstein, Ludwig, 21, 110

Yeats, W. B., 32, 60

Zola, Émile, 34

www.ingramcontent.com/pod-product-compliance
Lightning Source LLC
Chambersburg PA
CBHW030143240426
43672CB00005B/246